The Myths of Management

T0314275

For Alison, of course

Adrian Furnham is author of:
The Economic Mind
The Protestant Work Ethic
Personality at Work
Consumer Profiles
Biodata
Corporate Assessment
Business Watching
Why Psychology
The New Economic Mind

The Myths of Management

Forty Fables From The World of Management

Adrian Furnham

Whurr Publishers Ltd
London

First published 1996 by
Whurr Publishers Ltd
19b Compton Terrace, London N1 2UN, England

British Library Cataloguing-in-Publication Data
A catalogue record for this book is available from the
British Library.
ISBN: 978-1-897635-98-8

Contents

Foreword

Introduction

Being a manager isn't easy. I have been an academic, a consultant and a manager and I know the latter is the most difficult.

People are more fickle, capricious and demanding than machines. That is what makes them simultaneously fascinating and infuriating. Most managers lead lives of quiet desperation. Few are trained in the skills, techniques and theories of management. Most are simply promoted to managerial rank and told to get on with it.

The philosophy of 'throwing people in at the deep end' and requiring them to become managers without any training is based on three completely wrong assumptions:

- First, that management is simply the application of common sense, which by definition everyone has, so should be quite straightforward. How, one wonders, can one account not only for completely different, indeed contradictory management theories and techniques but for people who after many years remain poor at it? Being a good manager is not simply the application of common sense! It takes knowledge, skill and practice.
- Second, it is often argued that employees have, over their careers, been exposed to good (and average and bad) managers themselves, and through simply observing their style, foibles, techniques and errors they could learn what to do: copy the good ones; avoid the problems of the bad ones. I watch a lot of tennis, but I am no player. Observation alone won't suffice.
- Third, the tough-minded, sink-or-swim, Darwinian types argue that managers-in-the-making soon rise to the challenge:

the good soon learn, the weak soon fail. The trial or proba-
tionary period is supposedly the time when managers have to
prove (or not) that they can do it. But how many fail to get
appointed? And indeed, what are the criteria of success or failure? As long as no major cock-ups occur (mass resignation, a
strike), most get the job.

Although one occasionally observes the bluff and bravado of a
supremely confident manager, few really good managers are
completely confident. Anyway, many psychologists would argue that
the bumptious know-all manager is actually behaving in this way to
cover up or compensate for his/her uncertainty or anxiety. Precisely
because management is multifaceted and difficult it is unlikely that
any manager should be cocksure. A changing workforce, new technology and new pressures mean new challenges always arise.

Of course, there are many good managers: fair, honest, farsighted etc., who lead happy, healthy, productive teams but they are
probably the exception rather than the rule.

So many managers, new and old, from all sorts of organisations
read books and magazines about management. Some volunteer for,
and others are unwilling conscripts on courses to teach them how to
manage better. Technology, societies and economic conditions
change, but people do not. In this sense the people skills and techniques of good management have probably not changed very much
for thousands of years. But other things have, and management is
about more than people.

Journalists, trainers and gurus have to deliver something *new*;
something that is a *breakthrough*; an idea; a method or technique
which turns the world on its head; and, what is more, is both infalli-
ble and totally necessary.

And so there are fads, fashions and folderols in popular management science. Old ideas have to be repackaged, reinvented, given new
names. Techniques both good and bad, like old soldiers, never really
die. They reappear in a new guise every so often with the promise of
solving all problems. And hence we have the modern myths of
management.

Myths

A myth, like a parable or an allegory, is a traditional story that
embodies popular beliefs or phenomena. Mythical means fanciful,
imaginary, fabricated, invented or imagined. People who mytholo-

gise either lack or ignore facts, telling stories and tales that have a tenuous, and increasingly reduced, link with reality. A myth-maker is a creator of myths or stories. And as they are retold, they become embellished, enlarged and hence more fanciful.

Myths are easy to identify when they recount extraordinary events and encounters between mythical beings (the impulsive accountant; the inexpensive lawyer) which defy normal conventions. Paradoxically it is argued that it is through these non-real events that great truths can be told – that myths proclaim great truths by telling great lies! But what do we do with contradictory myths – which one is correct?

Like dreams, myths have the ability to resolve ambiguities and conflicts. Put another way, one could say that myths paper over the cracks of reality. They rejoice in parsimony: short stories that convey much meaning. But like the psychologist's ink-blot they therefore become open to multiple meanings and therein lies their strength and weakness. Because they are so vague, so ambiguous, so unreal they can be used and abused in many ways.

And myths encourage rites and ritual. Indeed, myth is to ritual as music is to dance. Managers and management are curiously ritualistic. Any student of corporate culture, in fact anyone who has worked for a large variety of companies, knows of the sometimes odd rituals that people go through. Of course, they are not called rituals – they may be called corporate policy or departmental procedures, but they have all the characteristics of ritual.

Management ritual demarcates, emphasises, affirms and solemnises critical changes in social relationships. It is an industrial-strength, all-purpose solvent that regulates the business world.

Management myths are socially shared superstitions. They are passed on from generation to generation. And, despite considerable evidence to the contrary, they are believed and narrated for years and years, irrespective of the truthfulness of their content.

Management Myths

Myths and fables abound in management. The most interesting question is *why they arise*. Or, put another way, why don't they die?

Management myths could be equated with a *virus* that is passed on, possibly randomly. Or they could be seen as a *recessive gene*, inherited by those who take up the mantle of management. Some even see the cause of these myths as a *poisoned chalice*, passed on by succeeding generations of managers unable or unwilling to pass on their actual knowledge or experience.

But those dark analogies may be too crude. Myths are passed on through in-house stories of the past, corporate histories, management magazines and books. They are keenly discussed and eagerly devoured.

Much of management teaching and training is through case histories which are true-ish stories that, over time, develop into myths. Myths can be of *heroic* deeds by previous and current employees in one's own company and dastardly deeds by employees from other companies. Management myths function to help corporate identity; to help people use similar language and concepts in understanding both the past and the present; and in dictating when, why and what rituals should be enacted in the organisation.

If many management myths are, at best, only half-truths, the question remains: why do they endure? There are a number of related reasons why this is the case.

- *Lack of feedback*: Any training or change-related organisation knows people learn best by getting feedback on their performance. Ideally that feedback is SMART —Specific, Measurable, Achievable, Realistic and Trackable. Without feedback one has no idea of the effects of one's actions: good, bad or indifferent. Although most managers probably have an accounting and production feedback mechanism, most do not have systems (such as upward feedback) that provide them with information on how they are doing. Hence many continue to believe and enact management myths unaware of their drawbacks and limitations.

- *Superstitious behaviour*: This was discovered by a psychologist who, interested in the process of learning, had been teaching pigeons to perform various acts (peck at coloured levers, bob up and down to break a light beam). The training technique always supplied food after a correct response. One weekend he left the feeding machine on. Once a hour or so, for no apparent reason, it supplied food. Used to being rewarded for specific acts, the pigeons came to believe that what they were doing when they first received the welcome surprise was now the 'correct' response. So they continued. On the Monday morning when the researcher returned to the laboratory he found that, on the hour, the birds individually performed a strange ritual. Some pecked, other danced, some bobbed, some stretched out their wings, others marched purposefully around their cage. Shortly thereafter they received the food believing they had 'cracked the code'. The myth-believing manager is much the same. Believing themselves to have correctly observed the cause and effect of behaviour at work they perform strange and superstitious acts to achieve certain desired results. But because they have not realised the actual cause and determinants of the behaviour at work they seek to manage, they are strictly victims of superstitions.

• *Erratic education*: In nearly every country management education is patchy in terms of both quality and quantity. Some are expected to learn by observing their bosses, others to learn by trial and error. But this 'education' is pretty haphazard and often poor. Consequently, some managers copy the superstitious behaviour of their 'elders and betters' whilst others pick up myths from magazines whose function is more to entertain than educate. Sometimes the personal experiences and philosophy of a strong (authoritarian as well as charismatic) CEO can lead to whole organisations behaving in bizarre and myth-related ways. Management education – or lack of it – is a major cause of the perpetuation of myths.

• *Desperation*: Management is not easy, particularly in economically uncertain times. With the possibility of economic failure, the spectre of personal and personnel unemployment, and increasingly sophisticated customers and competitors, many managers become, quite naturally, pretty frantic. In this situation they tend to cling on to any hope, to follow any path and strategy that supposedly leads to success. The more radical and simple the solution (and, of course, equally the probability that it is wrong) the more attractive it becomes to the desperate manager. In this sense it is not gurus that sell myths but rather managers who buy them. Desperate people are willing to try anything. Hence myths flourish.

• *Uncertainty avoidance*: At the end of the twentieth century the speed of change (social, economic, technological) leaves many change-fatigued. Given the pain and difficulty of learning new skills, restructuring organisations, redefining the roles of customers and clients, many managers look back to a secure, but non-existent past. The past for many appears rosy, secure and stable and it seems that if one keeps doing things the 'old way' all will be well. Intolerant of ambiguity, unhappy with uncertainty, scared by change, some managers cling to the beliefs of their 'fathers'. The past is another country where they do things differently: things which are not necessarily good or bad, helpful or unhelpful, adaptive or maladaptive. And hence old truths, which are in fact old lies, are perpetuated.

Snake-oil Salesman

Just as potential consumers and patients are constantly bombarded with 'new and miraculous' alternative (or complementary) therapies, potions and techniques, so the poor, stressed manager is frequently offered novel management methods.

Many are encouraged to adopt 'liberation management', to do 'organisational re-engineering' or even to embrace 'the Zulu principles' as the new way to corporate nirvana. Older, more established management practices must, it seems, be dispensed with. That old favourite 'mushroom management', where workers are kept in the dark and have corporate manure shovelled on them, must go. An acceptance of the new seems to demand a complete rejection of the old. It may be that people take up 'alternative' management precisely for the same reason that people choose complementary medicine. It is such things as lower back pain that drive the GP's patient into the arms (literally) of the complementary practitioner. There is nothing like a *chronic* condition, incurable by general practitioners or specialists and their rocket-science technology, to drive the helpless, hapless and hopeless patient to seek an alternative to conventional medicine.

Moreover, the complementary or alternative practitioners are warm, calming, therapeutic people who give you plenty of time because they are 'interested in the whole person'. Because there is nothing quite as interesting as ourselves, most of us are easily seduced into talking and disclosing various well-guarded secrets.

Most people are not pulled by the attraction of complementary medicine but *pushed* by the failure of orthodox medicine. They are hooked by the soothing balm and personal touch of the alternative practitioner which stands in strong contrast to the cold, technical and all-too-brief interview with the GP.

Consider now the harassed, battered, CEO of a small British company desperately trying to keep afloat against strong competition. He or she knows that it is only on good management of the committed employees that survival, let alone success, depends. And yet traditional management techniques of carrot and stick, even of performance management, do not seem to be working.

Like back pain, managerial and employee incompetence seem to be chronic. And nothing much appears to change this: the disciplinary interview, a freeze on wage increases, seminars on the Nipponese, Teutonic even Gallic threat – all seem unable to do the trick. The high technology of management, such as the spreadsheet, the appraisal form, and the performance-related pay calculations, do not cure the chronic problem.

So when the guru of alternative management comes along, the desperate manager pays attention. No longer smelling of snake oil, the alternative management gurus, like the complementary medical practitioners, are polished, well dressed and sophisticated. In fact they ape many of the practices and have similar tools to their ortho-dox and traditional colleagues. They may have the portable PC, tele-phone and fax. They probably have impressive-looking certificates showing less well-known qualifications from the University of the Watford Gap and – most importantly - they exude confidence.

Like the complementary medical practitioners, the gurus or consultants of alternative management are interested in the *whole* business. They encourage the 'chronic sufferer', in this case the exas-perated manager, to pour out his or her woes about all, and every, aspect of the business. They welcome the opportunity to counsel and it may be some time before they reveal their particular solution.

The tarot cards, the crystals and the essential oils of alternative management take various forms. They may involve complete restructuring of the organisation, 'commitment workshops', or the pairing of mentors with subordinates.

The placebo effect works well for alternative management advo-cates but, like all placebos, its effects wear off and the chronic prob-lem returns. It is a sad fact that most alternative management, like most complementary medicine, is bogus, fraudulent and wrong. The principles on which it is based simply do not work in the long run.

One American consultancy called itself Lazarus because it attempted to bring back companies from the dead. Some consultants and gurus certainly provide wacky ideas. Tom Peters told us to 'cele-brate heroes and forget zeros'. Others demanded Japanese-style military PT before work. Curiously, some of the ideas and recom-mendations of the alternatives stick in the management lexicon, but others are soon jettisoned.

Yesterday's heresy can become today's orthodoxy. But a lot of the seed of alternative management falls by the wayside. What did happen to T groups? Management must hope that the Darwinian principle of the survival of the fittest means that what is good in alter-native management gets picked up and that which is not is appropri-ately junked.

The following myths are varied in terms of who believes them, how strongly they are held, how much actual truth there is in them. But they are pretty widely held and potentially dangerous.

It is the aim here as much to entertain as educate. To take a sideways look at the fact and fiction in management science; to turn cynics and naive hopefuls into critical sceptics; to find the pith and reject the myth; to understand the differences between sense and nonsense; and to increase the able in management by exposing the fable.

Adrian Furnham
Islington, London 1995

Chapter 1: Myths about Motivation

- Too many people quit looking for work when they find a job.
- People who work sitting down get paid more than people who work standing up (Ogden Nash).
- What counts is not the number of hours you put in, but how much you put in the hours.
- If you do anything just for money you don't succeed (B. Hearn).
- The basic task of management is to make people productive (Peter Drucker).
- The worst mistake a boss can make is not to say 'Well done' (John Ashcroft).

Ask any manager about his major problems and it is unusual not to hear the word motivation. It is a vague term, of course, and therefore easily abused but what managers often mean is ensuring that employees work at maximum performance with minimum interference.

What all employers want is the able, dedicated employee who derives pleasure from their work well done. The intrinsically motivated, competent employee in fact does not really need a manager except for guidance and feedback. That is because the work itself – or features associated with it such as the company of other workers or the quality of the end-product – is itself sufficiently rewarding to most employees who will happily work for that end alone.

But much work is dull and requires little skill. How, then, can we best motivate people: money, the prospect of promotion, praise? It is not only a matter of *getting* employees promoted but also of *keeping* them at it! The latter is no doubt more important than the former because just as salt loses its flavour so the power and impact of rewards lessen over time.

Myths abound where issues are complex. Simple solutions are

frequently offered which may be part right but insufficient or equally frequently all wrong. Much debate concerns the power of reward, particularly the power of money. Not only is money a very short-term solution but it can, quite contrary to plan, demotivate!

Various reward or motivation 'systems' have been tried but fail not so much because of their inherent characteristics but rather the way they are applied. They require planning, investment and good management...and it is the latter that is the most frequent cause of failure. A bad manager blames his performance management system in precisely the same way as a bad workman blames his tools.

There are subtle ways of motivating staff. Indeed many are self-fulfilling. Managers often communicate more than they know or expect to their staff which can have powerful consequences on their motivation. Again it is about implicit rather than explicit factors.

Some people are quite simply more motivated than others. This is self-evidently true but, apart from selecting the most motivated, is there anything the manager can do? The answer is inevitably yes and it concerns specifically the employees' sense of control over their destiny, which can be a simple but powerful motivating experience. It is one of the messages of empowerment.

1. Money is the Best Work Motivator

Academics, management gurus and front-line managers don't always agree. Often they don't like or respect each other, and occasionally the latter, the people at the coal-face, simply disagree with those in the ivory tower.

One topic that never goes away is money, and more importantly its ability to motivate the average worker. Hard-bitten middle managers, particularly if they are Chinese, believe money is the most powerful motivator. Paradoxically, it is nearly always those who do not have it in their power to motivate by monetary rewards who believe this to be the case. And, by contrast, the people who have control over the purse strings may not regard money as very relevant.

Does money motivate people? Is money, the poor people's credit card, a consistent and powerful motivator of work performance? What of economic motivation?

Classical organisation theorists assumed that workers had to be driven to work by the carrot and the stick, which may often have been true during the Industrial Revolution. A similar view has been taken by most economists, with their concept of 'economic man'.

Occupational psychologists reacted very strongly to these views, and in some books failed to discuss economic incentives at all. The psychologists cite support from surveys in which workers were asked which factors were most important in making a job good or bad: 'pay' commonly came sixth or seventh after 'security', 'co-workers', 'interesting work', 'welfare arrangements'. This has been confirmed in more recent surveys which have found that pensions and other benefits are valued more than salary alone.

The basic psychology of incentives is that behaviour can be influenced if it is linked to some desired reward. Speed of work is an example. There is little doubt that people work harder when paid by results than when paid by the time they put in.

Other studies have shown the effects of an incentive plan for reducing absenteeism, which fell immediately as soon as the plan was introduced, and rose again when it was discontinued. There is also evidence that money can act as an incentive for people to stay with their organisation.

In a Pay for Performance system performance may be measured by piecework, group piecework, measured day work or performance/merit appraisal and 'pay' may include profit sharing. Often the competitiveness that characterises these systems causes problems.

But the simple fact is that money is but one motivator. Job security, a pleasant environment, a considerate boss are all motivators as well. Consider the following: Would you prefer £1000 (tax free) or a week's extra holiday? £1000 or a new job title? £5000 or a job guarantee for life? £1000 or meaningful and intrinsically satisfying work? Put like that, as a choice between money alone and other motivators, the power of money declines.

If, indeed, money *is* a powerful motivator or satisfier at work, why has research consistently shown that there is no relationship between wealth and happiness? In fact there are four good reasons why this is so:

- *Adaptation*: although everybody feels 'happier' after a pay rise, windfall or pools win, one soon adapts to this and the effect very rapidly disappears.
- *Comparison*: people define themselves as rich/wealthy by comparing themselves with others. However, with increased wealth, people usually move in more 'up-market' circles where there is always someone wealthier than themselves.
- *Alternatives*: as economists say, the declining marginal utility of money means that as one has more of the stuff, other things

such as freedom and true friendship seem much more valuable.

- *Worry*: an increased income is associated with a shifting of concern from money issues to the more uncontrollable elements of life (e.g. self-development), perhaps because money is associated with a sense of control over one's fate.

Money doesn't always bring happiness. People with £10 million are no happier than people with only £9 million. Yes, everyone wants more money. Economists – the dismal scientists – are right: money does act as a work motivator, but to a large extent in the short term, for some workers more than others, and at a cost often to the morale of the organisation. And psychologists are also correct: money is only one of many motivators of behaviour.

The main value of money is that one lives in a world in which it is overestimated. It doesn't buy friends? No, merely a better class of enemy. The accumulation of money does not end people's troubles, it merely changes them.

The power of money as a motivator is short-lived. Further, in countries with high taxation it is often less attractive than tangible goods. In addition, it has less effect the more comfortable people are. Yet it may be particularly important in times or places of political (even economic) instability because it is highly portable. Camus was right when he said it is a kind of spiritual snobbery to believe people can be happy without money. But, given or earning a modest, average amount, the value of other work benefits become greater.

2. Always Reward Good Performance

Some jobs and some tasks are intrinsically satisfying. That is, by their very nature they are interesting and pleasant to do. They can be enjoyable for a wide variety of reasons and much depends on the preference, predilections and propensities of individuals.

Intrinsic satisfaction implies that merely doing the job is, in itself, its own reward. Therefore, for such activities no reward and no management should be required. But the naive manager might unwillingly destroy this ideal state of affairs.

Take the case of the academic writer scribbling at home on a research report. The local children had for three days played extremely noisily in a small park near his study and, like all noise of this sort, it was highly stressful because it was simultaneously loud, uncontrollable and unpredictable. What should be done? (1) Ask (politely) them to quieten down or go away. (2) Call the police or the parents if you know them. (3) Threaten them with force if they do not comply. (4) All of the above in that order.

The wise don used none of the above. Unworldly maybe but, as someone whose job depended on intrinsic motivation, the academic applied another principle. He went to the children on the fourth morning and said, somewhat insincerely, that he had very much enjoyed them being there for the sound of their laughter, and the thrill of their games. In fact, he was so delighted with them that he was prepared to pay them to continue. He promised to pay them each £1 a day if they carried on as before.

The youngsters were naturally surprised but delighted. For two days the don, seeming grateful, dispensed the cash. But on the third day he explained that because of a 'cash flow' problem he could only give them 50p each. The next day he claimed to be 'cash light' and only handed out 10p.

True to prediction the children would have none of this, complained and refused to continue. They all left in a huff promising never to return to play in the park. Totally successful in his endeavour, the don retired to his study luxuriating in the silence.

This parable illustrates a problem for the manager. If a person is happy doing a task, for whatever reason, but is also 'managed' through explicit rewards (usually money), the individual will tend to focus on these rewards, which then inevitably have to be escalated to maintain satisfaction. This is therefore a paradox: reward an intrinsically motivated person by extrinsic rewards and he/she is likely to become less motivated because the nature of the motivation changes. Unless a manager can keep up the increasing demands on the extrinsic motivator (i.e. constant salary increases) the person usually begins to show less enthusiasm for the job.

There is considerable research on the types of job which give their holders the most satisfaction. Contrary to popular predictions, it is not merchant bankers or high-flying company executives who report most satisfaction. Many in fact yearn for early but 'comfortable' retirement. Nor is it social workers, nurses or others in the care business. It turns out that craftsmen and women report most job satisfaction. The 'crafts' vary: mathematicians are very job satisfied, as are furniture makers. Goldsmiths, stone-wall builders, and other employed craftspeople report the highest intrinsic satisfaction. Even thatchers – no, not the blessed Margaret's brood – appear to enjoy their work.

Craftspeople have intrinsic job satisfaction partly because of the pace, timing and control they have in their work but also because of their identification with the final product. However, once a fine furniture builder becomes a successful businessman he may lose his thrill at design and carving. That is why the best craftspeople have 'agents' who deal with money matters. This is not only because the practitioners are frequently inexperienced at running a business but also many do not like this aspect, despite the obvious monetary rewards.

Intrinsic motivation in part explains why some people continue in poorly paid employment. They do not need motivating in the usual way – through an astute mixture of carrot and stick – because they are intrinsically motivated. But, like all of us, they still respond to praise for the product or service that they supply.

For those limited few who enjoy doing what they do, working (like virtue) is its own reward.

3. It is Better to Reward Organisational Loyalty than Personal Performance

Some companies have always had performance-related pay (Pay-For-Performance, or PFP). Nearly all sales forces rely heavily on it. Others have had it for a decade or more, particularly large American companies. Recently many British companies have embraced it voluntarily, whilst many public sector organisations are encouraged, then forced, screaming and resisting the whole way, to take it on board.

Does PFP work? Of course, it depends on what one means by work. Its aim is to boost both productivity and morale by introducing the concept of equity (rather than equality) at work, such that performance (not service or job description) is directly related to pay and it is unusual for any two people to receive the same pay.

There are different types of PFP system depending on who is included (to what level); how performance will be measured (objective counts, subjective ratings or a combination) and which incentives will be used (money, shares etc.). For some organisations the experiment with PFP has not been a success. Sold as a panacea for multiple ills it has backfired to leave a previously dissatisfied staff more embittered and alienated. There are various reasons for the failure of PFP systems.

First, there is frequently a poorly perceived connection between pay and performance. Many employees have inflated ideas about their performance levels which translate into unrealistic expectations about rewards. When thwarted, employees complain, and it is they who want the system thrown out.

Often the percentage of performance-based pay is too low, relative to base pay. That is, if a cautious organisation starts off with too little money in the pot, it may be impossible to discriminate between good and poor performance, so threatening the credibility of the whole system.

But the most common problem lies in the fact that, for many jobs, the lack of objective, relevant, countable results requires heavy, often exclusive use of performance ratings. These are very susceptible to systematic bias – leniency, halo etc. – which render them neither reliable nor valid.

Another major cause is resistance from managers and unions. The former, on whom the system depends, may resist these changes because they are forced to be explicit, to confront poor performance and tangibly to reward the behaviourally more successful. Unions always resist equity- rather than equality-based systems because the latter render the notion of collective bargaining redundant.

Further, many PFP plans have failed because the performance measure(s) which are rewarded were not related to the aggregated performance objectives of the organisation as a whole, that is to those aspects of the performance which were most important to the organisation. Also, the organisation must ensure that workers are capable of improving their performance. If higher pay is to drive higher performance, workers must believe in (and be capable of) performance improvements.

But PFP plans can work very well indeed, providing various steps are taken. First, a bonus system should be used in which merit (PFP) pay is not tied to a percentage of base salary but is an allocation from the corporate coffers. Next, the band should be made wide whilst keeping the amount involved the same: say 0–20% for lower paid employees and 0–40% for higher levels. Performance appraisal must be taken seriously by making management raters accountable for their appraisals; they need training, including how to rate behaviour (accurately and fairly) at work.

Information systems and job designs must be compatible with the performance measurement system. More importantly, if the organisation takes teamwork seriously, group and section performance must be included in the evaluation. It is possible and preferable to base part of an individual's merit pay on team evaluation. Finally, special awards to recognise major individual accomplishments need to be considered separately from an annual merit allocation.

Any PFP system must support the strategy and values of the organisation. If they emphasise entrepreneurial activity and independent effort they are all the more crucial. Closed, secretive, bureaucratic cultures do not take to PFP and they undermine it. Openness and trust must be apparent if employees are to accept the standards and believe in the equity of rewards. Clearly, rewards valued by the worker must be clearly linked to the outcomes valued and provided by the employers.

But for those who consistently rehearse the problems without the benefits of PFP perhaps one can shout 'TINA', as was the custom of Margaret Thatcher. 'There Is No Alternative', or, at least, none that is demonstrably more successful at improving performance and morale.

4. Some Managers Always Seem to be Assigned the Best People

Nearly 30 years ago an American educationalist demonstrated a well-known but frequently ignored fact. He compared the performance of equivalent pupils under two groups of teachers: those who had been led to believe their students were slow learners, and those who believed their children were of superior ability and capacity. Pupils in the latter group learnt faster. Children whose teachers expected them to succeed did better in all tests compared with those whose teachers had lower expectations of them. Of course, the expectations of the students themselves were important, but often these were a direct function of the teacher's expectations.

Careful studies of how expectations are communicated and affect performance showed a number of processes in operation. When their expectations were high, the teachers tended to teach qualitatively and quantitatively more new or novel material. They tended to pay closer attention, to give more clues to, and to allow longer responses from those whom they believed to be bright. The teachers also initiated and engaged in more interactions with high- than with low-expectation students. Finally, teachers tend to praise high-expectation students more, and proportionally more per correct response, whilst low-expectation students are criticised more, and proportionally more per incorrect response.

In short, different expectations lead to different treatments, which lead to different performances. The results of the research indicate quite clearly that:

- What managers expect of their subordinates and the treatment they are given largely determines performance and career progress.
- A unique characteristic of superior managers is their ability to create high performance expectations which subordinates fulfil.
- Less effective managers fail to develop similar expectations and, as a consequence, the productivity of their subordinates suffers.
- Subordinates, more often than not, appear to do what they believe they are expected to do.

A good illustration concerns the manager of an American insurance company. He had observed that outstanding insurance companies grew faster than average or poor ones, and that new insurance agents performed better in outstanding companies than in average or poor ones, regardless of their sales aptitude. He decided to group his superior agents in one unit to stimulate their performance and to provide a challenging environment in which to introduce new sales-people.

Accordingly, the manager assigned his six best agents to work with his best assistant manager, an equal number of average producers to work with an average assistant manager, and the remaining low producers to work with the least able manager. He then asked the superior group to produce two-thirds of the premium volume achieved by the entire agency the previous year. Although the productivity of the 'super-staff' improved dramatically, the productivity of those in the lowest unit actually declined and the attrition among them increased. The performance of the superior agents rose to meet their managers' expectations, whilst that of the weaker ones declined lamentably.

When salespersons are treated by their managers as talented, they try to live up to that image and do what they know superior salespersons are expected to do. But when the salespeople with poor productivity records are treated by their managers as having 'little chance' of success, this negative expectation also becomes a managerial self-fulfilling prophecy. Less successful salespersons have great difficulty maintaining their self-image and self-esteem. In response to low managerial expectations, they typically attempt to prevent additional damage to their egos by avoiding situations that might lead to greater failure. They either reduce the number of sales calls they make or avoid trying to 'close' sales when they might result in further painful rejection, or both. Low expectations and damaged egos lead them to behave in a manner which increases the probability of failure, thereby fulfilling their managers' prophecy.

How do managers develop the art of high expectations? The answer, in part, seems to be that superior managers have greater confidence than other managers in their *own* ability to develop the talents of their subordinates. Contrary to what might be assumed, the high expectations of superior managers are based primarily on what they think about themselves – about their own ability to select, train and motivate their subordinates. What managers believe about themselves subtly influences what they believe about their subordinates, what they expect of them and how they treat them. If they have confidence in their own ability to develop and stimulate them to high levels of performance, they will expect much of them and will treat them with confidence that their expectations will be met. But if they have doubts about their ability to stimulate their staff, they will expect less of them and will treat them with less confidence.

Put another way, the superior managers' record of success and confidence in their own ability give their high expectations credibility. As a consequence, their subordinates accept these expectations as realistic and try hard to achieve them. So it is true: nothing succeeds like success.

5. Success at Work is a Matter of Luck

How do you 'get on' in your organisation? Sheer ability and hard work? Luck in being in the right place at the right time? Sycophantic kow-towing to those in authority? Simple old-fashioned bribery?

To a large extent there are two contrasting attitudes and beliefs about the way in which work and indeed life's rewards and outcomes are determined. Some people believe we can neither predict nor influence significant events, whilst others believe we can. In psychobabble the former are called *fatalists*, the latter *instrumentalists*. More importantly, these beliefs are self-fulfilling.

Consider dental patients: essentially they can be categorised as *preventive* or *restorative*. Preventive patients tend to be instrumentalist. They believe that, given sufficient flossing and brushing, an adequate healthy diet and regular visits to the dentist/hygienist, dental health can be maintained. Recent research suggests that too-regular visits to the dentist might not, however, be such a good idea. Dentists are trained to drill, fill and bill and they need to perform the first to issue the last. Perhaps, like the ancient Chinese, one should only pay one's doctor when one is well. But that might increase the number of 'clean bills of health' on offer!

The restorative patient may be quite simply (and understandably) dentist-phobic and fearful of pain. They may also be poor, badly organised or uninterested in their dental health. But equally they may be fatalists who are convinced their dental health is a function of luck – genetic inheritance, the local water supply, eating habits as a child etc., over which they currently have no control. Hence they do nothing (or a minimal amount) to ensure dental health.

The same pattern is found in the workplace. There are those who believe they can control their destiny by effort and ability, by judicious politicking and by 'making their luck'. Instrumentalists believe in essence that their own actions produce outcomes. Hence they tend to work hard and are receptive to feedback and ways of becoming more efficient.

But there are those who believe that luck or 'powerful others' determine their occupational success. Fatalists tend to believe that outcomes are the result of random coincidences rather than of their own actions. Hence, they do not believe their own effort is relevant to their occupational success.

Studies over the past 30 years have revealed refreshingly unequivocal results supporting the arguement that instrumentalism is a cause and consequence of success and fatalism a cause and consequence of failure. Results show the following:

- *Motivation*: instrumentalists are more likely to believe that their efforts will result in good performance, and they exhibit stronger belief in their own competence.
- *Job performance*: instrumentalists perform better because of their greater effort; they seek more information in complex task situations, and exhibit greater personal career effectiveness.
- *Job satisfaction*: instrumentalists are more satisfied than fatalists (generally as well as in the job), partly because of their success.
- *Leadership*: instrumentalists prefer participative approaches from their supervisors, rely more on personal persuasion with their subordinates, and seem more task oriented and less socially oriented.
- *Job perception*: instrumentalists perceive more personal control over their environment, request more feedback on the job and perceive less role strain.
- *Turnover*: highly job-satisfied instrumentalists exhibit the same rate of turnover (presumably low) as fatalists but, for highly

dissatisfying jobs, instrumentalists exhibit more turnover than fatalists.

Why not test yourself? Circle True or False.

1. A job is what you make of it.   T/F
2. On most jobs, people can pretty much accomplish whatever they set out to accomplish.   T/F
3. If you know what you want out of a job, you can find a job that gives it to you.   T/F
4. If employees are unhappy with a decision made by their boss, they should do something about it.   T/F
5. Getting the job you want is mostly a matter of luck.   T/F
6. Making money is primarily a matter of good fortune.   T/F
7. Most people are capable of doing their jobs well if they make the effort.   T/F
8. In order to get a really good job you need to have family members or friends in high places.   T/F
9. Promotions are usually a matter of good fortune.   T/F
10. When it comes to landing a really good job, who you know is more important than what you know.   T/F
11. Promotions are given to employees who perform well on the job.   T/F
12. To make a lot of money you have to know the right people.   T/F
13. It takes a lot of luck to be an outstanding employee in most jobs.   T/F
14. People who perform their jobs well generally get rewarded for it.   T/F
15. Most employees have more influence on their supervisors than they think they do.   T/F
16. The main difference between people who make a lot of money and people who make little money is luck.   T/F

Score

1–4 (T) 5–6 (F) 7 (T) 8–10 (F) 11 (T) 12–13 (F) 14–15 (T) 16 (F)

Interpretation

0–6   A helpless fatalist. You *can* influence your life.
7–10   A moderate pessimist about control at work.
11–12 A healthy instrumentalist.
13+   A strong instrumentalist. Beware you don't believe that you (and your subordinates) are responsible for *everything.*

Instrumentalists are usually self-starters. They need positive reward and feedback like everybody else but because they believe effort results in performance which results in (intrinsic and extrinsic) reward they get on with it. Not everybody, of course, is under one's control, particularly if one works for a big organisation, and the strong instrumentalist may be deeply frustrated, even demotivated by discovering this.

It is fatalists who need managerial help. They are frequently not motivated because they don't see the consequences of their behaviour. They need a heavy dose of attentive management: they need to see and believe that the quality and quantity of the performance is noticed, measured and rewarded. And the experience of personal control can be deeply motivating in itself.

6. Tipping is a Good System for the Customer

It has been said that tipping started when gratuities were dropped into a box mark TIPS – to insure prompt service. However, much confusion and resentment surrounds this quaint habit. In the USA, though, tipping is institutionalised, organised and codified to a forbidding extent, and heaven help the naive person who breaks the unwritten rules.

In Europe, mystery and discomfort surround the rules. Thus, does one tip cloakroom (hat-check) attendants on depositing or retrieving clothes? If at the hairdressers there are specialist washers, stylists, colourists and cutters, who should be tipped? Will hotels at least give one the option of coping with one's own bags? If not, who is it to be tipped and when during the stay?

What is the meaning and function of tipping? Why does it exist? Why tip cabbies and hairdressers but not tailors? What are the determinants of tipping? And, most importantly, how does tipping affect the service-givers (e.g. waiters), the recipients (i.e. customers) and the relationship between the two parties?

Economists would no doubt argue (if they could agree) that tipping has a rational economic explanation. A tip is surely a payment for something extra (extra services or extra effort) beyond those specified as normal. Most people we tip provide services that are fairly difficult to measure, so his or her obligations and performance cannot be fully controlled. Hence the tip is the mechanism which complements the fixed market price where the sole commodity (i.e. service) contains non-standard or immeasurable components. But if this were true there would be a direct relationship between the size of the tip and the degree to which the performed service extended beyond normal duties in terms of speed, politeness etc. Whilst this may occasionally be the case, any waiter/ress will tell you that the size of the tip (if not a standard amount) is a function of such things as size of the dining party, the size of the bill, the need of the bill-payer to impress his/her friends. So much for an economic explanation which at any rate cannot account for the fact that some tipping is genuinely altruistic and, as far as I know, beyond economists who always posit self-interest!

Sociologists, on the other hand, see the tip as a gift. Because the recipient of a service feels gratitude or indebtedness to the provider, he or she leaves a tip as a gift supplementary to the bill. This free giving becomes a way of establishing and maintaining social status and power over somebody. It is significant that in several different languages the word gift means poison. The recipients of a service (the customers) get more than they pay for (in terms of service) which motivates them to reciprocate or discharge obligations and thereby balance the account. If they fail to do so, they will be under pressure to repay with social approval or subordination (or a mixture). Further, if the customer tips more than the person deserves, this superiority is established beyond any doubt because the balance tips in the donor's favour. Thus, paradoxically, the tip is not an expression of gratitude but a defence against gratitude. Tipping is a form of social control!

But is it true that tipping can be a demonstration of dominance and superiority? In some languages (such as Dutch and German) the tip contains a derogatory element implying that the money will be used for drink or some other improper purpose. Frequently waiters and cabbies talk of the humiliation involved in tipping, though I appear to have met an equally large number who are humiliated by the lack of a tip!

The trouble with both sociological and economic explanations is that they both assume an 'ongoing' as opposed to a 'one-off' encounter. Most frequently one tips those one never sees again. Both assume that people tip as an investment in future service but studies have shown the opposite: regular repeat-trade customers tip *less* than irregulars. Also tipping is not frequently done publicly as a display of rank and power. It is characterised by privacy and discretion. Many recipients deliberately don't look at the amount until well after the transaction.

Psychologists, on the other hand, agree that tipping is a form of ego massage calculated to enhance the self-image of the tipper. Also, by giving a tip – above and beyond the agreed or set price – the tipper can demonstrate that he/she is not fully trapped by market forces and can be capable of voluntary, discretionary action. The tip can sometimes be seen as a result of the customer's insecurity or anxiety. A maid or hairdresser deserves a tip through having access to the customer's private territory or articles that may just pose a threat to the customer's public face. The tip can buy their server's silence because it buys loyalty or indebtedness. Psychologists stress that tipping is intrinsically motivated rather than performed for the sake of external material or social rewards.

Enough academic speculation! At any rate, nearly all restaurants now include the tip, i.e. service charge, in the bill. This could be a manifestation of benevolence on the part of restaurateurs eager to see their staff get the gratuities they deserve (but don't get in their salaries). In fact the precise opposite is true. Where such people as waiters and waitresses get 'free-ranging' tips (like eggs) depending on their service, a good deal of conflict arises because they have different requirements from management and superiors on the one hand and customers on the other. If a server's tip is dependent on the customer's discretion, the latter has considerable power over the former. Consequently waitresses who receive discretionary tips tend to be more loyal to customers and adopt their views, which of course frequently brings them into considerable conflict with management (particularly the cooks).

So we now have the 'service charge' which managers prefer because it gives them more control and *can* be used to ensure equitable rewards for non-visible staff.

But there will always be those who will be inventive in their gratitude. Tony Hancock is said to have rewarded his cabbie with the following: 'Here, my man, is a tea-bag. Have a drink on me.'

Chapter 2: Myths about Training

- If you think education is expensive, try ignorance (Derek Bok).
- Experience is a good school. But the fees are high.
- The great advantage of the sort of education that I had was precisely that it made practically no mark upon those subjected to it (Malcolm Muggeridge).
- God help those who train themselves (Lord Young).
- The mark of a true MBA is that he is often wrong but seldom in doubt (Robert Buzzell).
- We have, in my opinion, too many undergraduates taking arts courses and then doing a thesis on Sanskrit or the influence of Madrigals in Elizabethan society instead of teaching people the art of modern management (Lord Stokes).

Few people arrive at a job fully trained. Even the most technically competent professional usually requires some initial training. And because of the speed of development in certain technical fields most employees – and managers – require regular training. Training may be required because of changes in technology, process or product. It may be a simple update on upgraded technology or may require the complete relearning (or even worse unlearning) of new methods.

Because it is true that the only constant is change, employees and managers need to have their knowledge and skill increased at regular intervals. Training is not only necessary but can be motivational. It can be boring or interesting, central or peripheral, effective or not.

Should training be sporadic and in response to specific need, or continual? Should it be like the gates of hell – broad– or should it be related to specific issues and skills? Continuing management education takes the broad and general approach whereas the short course takes the opposite. Both may be effective for different reasons. Yet few organisations can afford or genuinely have the sort of people who take serious continuing and continuous education.

For many managers, particularly those trained at a university, the distinction between education and training is not clear. Most organisations want educated managers and trained staff. The nature of the two differs in a number of ways. They are simply different – neither superior nor inferior – and therefore have quite different consequences.

The efficacy of training depends as much on the type, syllabus, timing and place of the training as the style and preference of the trainer. Most people have been deeply influenced by individual teachers they remember with affection and gratitude. Equally we can all remember the teacher (trainer, instructor) whose manner and style put us off a topic for all time. There is quite often a 'fit' between the trainer and his/her material – indeed people with different skills and personalities are attracted to quite different types of training course. But even within the same area their approaches may be radically different.

Just as trainers differ quite considerably so do those attending courses. This is not only the distinction between volunteers and conscripts but the attitudes delegates have to the whole business of training and learning. Trainers become highly sensitive to these differences, as well they might, because they are quite clearly related to not only how much the delegates learn but how they behave on courses.

Equally, some employees enthusiastically and voluntarily accept and embrace innovation and change. But whilst some technophiles seek out the nearest equipment and love courses that help them to use it, others shun it and have to be cajoled or forced.

Often training and management learning are done through case histories and stories. The latter are certainly not always true but does it matter? Case histories of competitor companies are interesting. They are also memorable and can very usefully highlight simple but important truths about one's own organisation.

But, faced with the cost of training – particularly if it is regular or even continuous, the manager is quite entitled to ask: does it work? This is a difficult question to answer, partly because of the definition and measurement of 'working'. Does a driving licence prevent accidents? Does psychotherapy make patients better? Probably ... but these are very difficult to prove. However, it may be much easier to explain why training does not work and there is no shortage of explanations as to why so many organisations shoot themselves in the foot.

7. You Learn about Management on the Job

The world of medicine has long been interested and concerned about continuing management education (CME). The reason is obvious: though all doctors have experienced a long, difficult and demanding training, once it ends and they become qualified, licensed professionals, they may lose touch with important developments. In a fast-changing world, they start becoming out of date the day they qualify.

The avuncular Dr Findlay image might be comforting and reassuring if all you want is Vick rubbed on your chest, but positively dangerous if you have a complicated and recently diagnosed virus. Important discoveries, new ways of treating illnesses and of being diagnostically sensitive to early signs of major diseases may pass by the hard-working doctor. So medics try hard to encourage continuing medical education in order to keep the profession up-to-date and to stress the point that education does not end on graduation.

Does the same happen to the MBA graduate? Is the Institute of Directors in favour of CME for managers? If so, what does this CME look like? What does a finance director or a marketing director need to know and how will he/she acquire that knowledge? Will reading the *Financial Times* and *Marketing Weekly* suffice? Or is the in-house training course a good source of education?

Management, like medicine, changes and develops. Some of these changes are fashion-based, others economically driven, but some reflect real developments in the discipline. Expensive, inefficient, unreliable and painful methods are discarded. Just as card files were replaced by computers, which took some mastering, so older methods of management are jettisoned in favour of better ways of doing things.

Most of us have at some time encountered a curious, neo-Dickensian world of management alive and well in a time-capsule, insulated against the modern world. Quaint and fascinating they may be; efficient they rarely are. Sir John Harvey-Jones's celebrated TV programmes were eloquent exposures of British companies which the world has passed by.

If one believes in CME in principle, there are inevitably 'what' and 'how' questions: What needs to be taught? How is one best educated? What does the hard-pressed, reactive, modern manager need to know through CME?

Continuing management education should be providing three things: knowledge, skills and attitudes. Business schools and universities prioritise them thus, but professionals stress skills first, the right attitude next and knowledge last. Despite the debate over priorities, most would agree that all three are important. Knowledge is essential. There is nothing as practical as good theory. Knowledge liberates – it teaches people to know how to ask questions, evaluate answers and solutions and, more prosaically, where to look for an answer. Putting knowledge into practice by the use of skills is also crucial. Language skills, computer skills and people skills provide for the efficient application of a knowledge base. But skills training without a good knowledge background turns out operators and technicians, not professionals. Equally important is the socialisation that Americans call 'attitude'.

Many employers complain most about the attitude of young, thrusting, MBA-touting graduates: too much knowledge, too few skills but, worst of all, a bad attitude. They are perceived as being arrogant, selfish and unworldly. Equally, the middle-aged, middlebrow, middle manager may be seen as cynical, sceptical, conservative and against change. Neither naive optimism nor cynical pessimism about education and change are appropriate. But one should not underestimate the socialising power of education. Business and medical schools know this. They are just as much about inculcating an attitude to work as providing knowledge and skills.

The next, just as relevant, CME question is not what to teach but how to teach it. Seminars, lectures, videos, homework exercises, mini-MBAs, shadowing others? There are many different educational methods, but they can be categorised. For instance, one dimension is the *speed* at which they aim to work: fast vs slow. Second, the breadth of their *impact* can be broad or narrow. The traditional academic education via lectures and book reading is slow and narrow: ideal for in-depth knowledge, carefully acquired, of a particular issue. A slow method aimed at a broad effect is group learning: groups which meet on a regular basis, perhaps with specific rules to explore issues together. Groups often learn more about the members' and group's dynamics than anything else but that, of course, may be the purpose.

A fast and narrow method may be expensive and often involves hiring a specialist to give an update. This means a careful and thorough review of the state of the art, and an analysis of recent trends, issues and debates. A fast method with a broad effect is the video-based skills development method. The short course can be highly effective for the quick acquisition of a broad perspective.

But beware the fast and broad. As the Bible says, the way to doom and destruction is broad and the way to enlightenment narrow. Different methods serve different purposes. They have different costs in every sense of the word. The traditional talk from a well-prepared and competent lecturer may serve the educational purpose best in one situation, whereas the slick videos, copied to each member of the organisation, may equally well serve a different purpose.

Continuous management education in knowledge, skills and attitudes is surely important. Equally it is crucial to find the best method for the task. To some extent the medium is the message. Clearly an astute fit between the two is necessary for CME.

People who advocate CME need to be questioned closely. Voltaire said the Holy Roman Empire was neither Holy nor Roman nor Empire. Similarly, continuing management education is rarely continual or continuous; it is not often for or about management; and it may be more like entertainment or punishment than education.

8. Teaching and Training are Essentially the Same

What is the difference between teaching students and training managers? It is not so much the fact that students tend to be young and immature whereas adults are, well, less so, or that students tend to be taught in institutions (such as universities and colleges), because adults are also taught in institutions (namely business premises or hotels), but rather the philosophy and feel of the two enterprises is so different.

As a 'compare and contrast' exercise, two groups/tasks at polar opposites have deliberately been set out to accentuate their differences. It is probably the case that in certain instances these differences are not marked or noticeable and may even cross over. But by and large the gulf remains wide.

One difference lies in the *spirit* and ultimate aim of the two enterprises. The one aim is to teach; the other to train. In academic courses, students are taught theory, first principles and abstract understanding. Their teachers are concerned that they understand the background and the theory behind what they are learning. The learning is frequently abstract without any obvious purpose except to deepen understanding of processes, procedures and principles.

But for managers, the training in a particular topic is nearly always practical and concrete. Value for money demands the speedy acquisition of a skill. Background details, historical origins, and theoretical models get jettisoned rapidly in favour of practical understanding and doing skills. 'Training effectiveness' is defined as the speed and cost by which managers acquire relevant skills, not the extent to which they understand theoretical concepts.

Teaching students, even in applied courses, remains context independent in the sense that they are rarely taught for a specific organisation. Doctors, dentists, accountants, even lawyers are taught their subjects with the knowledge that they may take their skills and practise in a multitude of contexts. Hence abstract concepts are more useful because they generalise better. But management training, particularly if it is organisationally sponsored, is highly context specific. Adults are trained in the house style, using the unique house concepts and language. Curiously it is frequently a source of pride to organisations that training is so context specific: they believe it provides a source of unity, is highly efficient and the degree to which it can be applied elsewhere is irrelevant. Anyway, organisations don't feel they should do the training for other businesses, for fear that employees would use them as cheap sources of excellent training.

The time frame of the two enterprises is very different. Academics tend to take a longer view of things. They resist being rushed, know relatively few time deadlines and tend to be (erroneously) very tolerant of students who fail to get work done on time. They argue that great work takes time; ideas have to mature. This stands in sharp contrast with the time-obsessed manager, newly returned from a time management course. Managers know they live in flux and the world is a capricious, ever-changing place. Hence the shelf life of ideas and methods is short and thus training must be for the here and now. Trainers use topical examples, are conscious of fashion and like to boast about being up-to-date, state-of-the-art users of both ideas and technology.

Students are expected to be disciplined, inner directed and self-initiated. Facilities and resources such as libraries and computers are provided, but students are expected to be enterprising self-starters who seek out more or better resources. A friend of mine from a management training school once described her one-year university postgraduate course as the most expensive reading list in the world! Management trainees expect and receive all the materials they need for the topic because time is short, and it is considered the job of the trainers to compile the study aids. There are often many workbook examples. Sophisticated materials and up-to-date technology are available for the trained, not the taught!

Academics are cautious, critical, sceptical (even cynical) sort of people. Many are intellectually phlegmatic, muted in their enthusiasm. They take a long time to be convinced of things and are trained to be questioning and doubting. Students have literary criticism; managers literary appreciation. Only theologians are taught apologetics – others get criticism. Trainers, on the other hand, are rewarded for, and themselves reward high levels of enthusiasm and certainty. Their role models, the 'gurus', know the answers, are certain about the solution, believe in the theory. They persuade by personal conviction, much like a religious converter. Indeed, training is evangelical: it is frequently made out to be fun and its benefits are praised.

Teaching students is a verbal process. This is not to say that diagrammatic models, formulae and charts are not used but rather they are more frequently used to summarise and illustrate. Academics try to understand the process or mechanism which may or may not be easily open to illustration. But the medium, like the message, is verbal and abstract, too complex and subtle for easily comprehensible slides.

Trainers, conversely, are frequently highly reliant on elaborate, often multicoloured slides. They love 'models' which are pretty pictures that 'illustrate' their point. How and why things are categorised or boxed in a particular way is rarely spelt out. Pictures are used to simplify, categorise and render easily memorable, and frequently contain cartoons and other jokes. Sometimes amusing terms are used to facilitate memory.

Pilots talk of bad flying as all thrust and no rudder; driving instructors of bad pupils as all accelerator and no gears; and sceptical teachers of courses as all style and no content. Often academic lectures may contain excellent content delivered in a dry, unappealing lecturing style. A lecture has been described as a process whereby the notes of the lecturer become the notes of the students without passing through the minds of either! A monotonous delivery with no pacing and no light and dark is frequently the lot of the undergraduate – competent, sometimes brilliant content, spoilt by unsophisticated delivery and presentation style.

Management trainers, on the other hand, always demonstrate a polished, modern, sophisticated style. Slides, videos, even role-plays are carefully prepared, and there is variety, amusing stories and a good pace. But frequently the content or the substance suffers at the hands of the performance. The trainer prefers easy access to ideas and the teacher the comprehensiveness of the course.

Some will no doubt strongly object to this compare and contrast exercise, claiming how mislabelled they have been. Frequently when a distinction is made, one pole or type appears more attractive than the other and neither side will happily accept what they see as a slur on their educational activities.

As a result of this gulf the movement from one world to the other is neither common nor easy. The corduroyed don may not so easily be able to supplement his meagre stipend at training courses. Equally the dapper trainer may not easily acquire the cachet he or she hopes by teaching at the local university. The skills, style and outlook of these two activities sometimes clash dramatically.

So the best advice for the aspirant student of the trainer or teacher is *caveat emptor*: let the buyer not only beware but choose wisely.

Teaching students	—	*Training managers*
	Philosophy	
Theoretical/Abstract		Practical/Concrete
	Aim	
Understanding		Doing
	Context	
Context-independent		Context-specific
	Time-frame	
Long-term, unlimited		Short-term, immediate
	Resources	
Self-initiated		Provided
	Tone	
Criticism/Sceptical		Enthusiasm/Zealous
	Medium	
Verbal/Processes		Diagrammatic/Models
	Values	
Content		Style

9. Most Management Trainers are Much the Same

Corporate education and training bills are significant. Most organisations realise that you cannot promote people to supervisory or managerial levels without teaching them *how* to manage. Other

organisations like to socialise or 'induct' their new employees into
the values, norms and myths of the corporate culture. Still others
inherit a pretty uneducated staff who really need a short-sharp-shock
training in accountancy, strategic planning or computer literacy.

Personnel or human resource departments which usually take
responsibility for education and training have the choice of developing an in-house training department or bringing in consultants/
trainers or both. This decision is based partly on history, partly on
the number of people who have to be trained (as a function of organisational size and staff turnover rates), partly on the money available
and partly on the experience of the human resources (HR) director.

Course junkies who have attended a variety of programmes have
seen various trainers at work. Naturally they come in all shapes and
sizes, have different styles and preferences. And it is also true that
there is often a good fit between the content of the programme and
the style of the presenter. However, clear categories of trainer styles
are in evidence.

- *The Evangelist Game Show Host:* These trainers are often vacu-
  ously extrovert show-offs. They believe the course is about
  having fun, winning prizes and 'believing'. The programmes
  are all about the showing and sharing of emotions. The evangelist in them feels the need to convert the delegates to their
  way of thinking, their models and their methods. They are
  often exhausting to be around, and definitely not the choice of
  the quiet, serious-minded participant.
- *The Academic Guru:* He or she is the talking head of the training
  business. Often they have a touch of arrogance and let you feel
  that all this is slightly beneath them. Some patronise the audi-
  ence, others drone on ignoring the perplexed and puzzled
  looks of the delegates. The guru in them is often the dangerous
  element because they may genuinely believe they have found
  the Holy Grail of management.
- *The Therapeutic Doctor:* Some trainers like to give the message
  'Trust me, I am a doctor' or 'Put your faith in me, I am experienced'. They try to cultivate the air of the wise 'Dr Findlay' of
  the market-place who has seen it all before and knows how
  people behave. This front can, of course, always serve as a way
  of diverting attention from the fact that he or she really has no
  data or research evidence upon which to base the theories
  expounded.
- *The Belittling Assassin:* Some trainers revel in their power to

expose and humiliate the powerful and the great-and-good, whatever their personal ability, skill or indeed history. They belong to the Dame Edna school of picking on hapless, and then helpless, victims of the course. Sometimes put up to it by senior management but often at random, these missiles in a course can do great psychological damage.

- *The Bullshitter/Facilitator:* For those who have precious little knowledge or skill, or simply those who have done no preparation, there is always the fall-back position of the facilitator. In essence this means others (the course participants) do the work. The bullshitter simply encourages them, by a variety of methods, not only to diagnose their own problems but to solve them on the course, and then takes the credit for the solution.
- *The Manual-dependent Schoolmarm:* Some trainers are rendered guideless, speechless and powerless if their slides and manuals are removed from them. Theirs is the 'open your textbooks to page 1' approach. Participants are simply required to complete a series of pre-ordained exercises that are supervised and inspected by the strict nanny-teacher. This is the serious and rather boring world of skill acquisition.
- *Mind-expander and Creative:* Occasionally one finds the trainer who has taken his or her de Bono rather too seriously. They believe it is their job to think 'laterally' on all occasions; to come up with radical, albeit impractical, alternatives. They may do this through brainstorming exercises or public free associations, but the outcome is the same.

The world of the professional consultant and trainer is a strange one and this, in part, helps generate the odd characters in the field. Often, because they are both well paid and well treated by their client organisations, they come to believe that what they say is profound, whilst those who adopt the seagull management style (fly in, shit all over everybody, fly out) never see the consequences of their advice and may delude themselves that it is inevitably/always useful. For the cynic it is a case of 'Those who can do; those who can't train; those who can't train, train trainers; whilst those who can't train trainers become management consultants'.

10. Everyone Dislikes and Resists Management Training

Most organisations make some investment in training their staff in management techniques. They either hire training consultants or staff an in-house department (or both) and usually send managers on external training courses in addition. The courses come in various packages with different titles. There are the skill-based courses, teaching such topics as negotiation, presentation, social or time-management skills. Others on offer are development workshops, customer-focused programmes and modified business-school courses.

Just as people come to resemble their dogs, so trainers seem to have personalities that fit their courses. The tutor for the course on self-presentation is immaculate; the trainer on the 'customer-driven' programme is exceptionally attentive to your needs; and the 'finance course for non-financial managers' lecturer is highly numerate. But what about the people who attend training courses? Why are they there? How do they react? Many experienced, full-time trainers tend to develop simple typologies to describe training course attenders or 'dellys' (delegates). Cabin crew, waitresses, nurses, traffic wardens and all those who deal with the general public as their customers tend to classify people into different groups (with sometimes unflattering labels). It is a shorthand to characterise the large numbers of individuals whom they encounter.

These typologies, of course, pigeon-hole people. They are prototypes that may never exist in pure form but which amuse the trainers who recognise their generic characteristics. They refer to the attitudes and behaviours of the delegates. Indeed they may also reflect the delegates' attitudes to their work.

- *The Prisoner:* The scowl on the face, the arms tightly folded across the chest, and the folded letter from the boss or personnel manager demanding (requiring) that they *have to* attend the course, characterise this type. They have probably succeeded at avoiding this course, or ones like it, many times before, but eventually are caught. They are prisoners: they don't want to be there and wish they were somewhere else. They are sour, negative, unhelpful and certainly uncooperative.
- *The Escapee:* This type is the course junkie who jumps at the opportunity at getting out of the office. They may hate their work or simply enjoy education and training at the company's expense. The escapee is usually rather too experienced at course activities, games and questionnaires and may well have done them before. They are easy to deal with from the trainer's point of view but not good value for money from the perspective of their company.

- *The Old Dog*: There are various reasons why some people believe they cannot be taught new tricks. Some delegates are on-the-job retirees, in the departure lounge of the organisation. They may in fact be quite a long way from retirement, but they are not interested in learning anything. Others believe courses are too abstract, too theoretical, too vague and have nothing to add to their day-to-day working lives.

- *The Eager Beaver*: This type comes in two forms. The first is the enthusiastic learner, genuinely interested in gaining skills, insights and knowledge. The second is the slightly naive delegate who is happy to take anything on board but has few critical facilities. This makes them too gullible and too unfocused, though certainly easy for the trainer.

- *The Intellectual*: Whereas the old dog may reject what he/she is told because it is too vague and theoretical, the intellectual wants to know the empirical and epistemological bases of the data being presented. Many are snobs who think they know more than the trainer (and sometimes do). These high flyers may believe either the content or the style is not appropriate for their level. They may enjoy humiliating the trainer if they can.

- *The Bastard*: Familiar to John Major, they are arrogant know-it-alls. They usually believe that personnel departments should be closed, all consultants fired, and the money put into the company's pension fund. In a curious way, they enjoy courses in the way they enjoy meetings, because they have learnt to be maximally disruptive. They may be simple attention-seekers and in some organisations are intellectually seriously underpowered. They are a nightmare for trainers because they are solely interested in scuppering or damaging the proceedings.

- *The Ingratiator*: Many people are anxious when attending courses because they fear being shown up in front of others. Those who fear being exposed as the product of the Peter Principle tend to be what Americans charmingly call 'Apple Polishers'. The ingratiator tries to do a deal with the trainer: 'I will be a good boy/good girl if you don't expose or humiliate me'. And for trainers it is a good deal.

Most trainers will probably recognise the above types, though they may use rather different categories or titles. And they also know that different companies tend to have more or less of each type. Thus the publicly-owned bureaucracy probably sends mainly old dogs, escapees and prisoners to courses, whereas the successful private company may send rather a lot of intellectuals and the occasional ingratiator.

Next time you're on a course, look around the room, and see who's in. But of course, you can play the same game with the trainers themselves. They too are equally pigeon-holeable. But that's another story.

11. Employees are Quick on the Uptake of Innovation

Perhaps the greatest testimony to the speed of technical innovation in the latter part of the twentieth century is the piles of redundant computers, many barely three years old, which are relegated to company cupboards and store rooms. They are soon replaced by shiny, smaller, even more powerful, colourful and user-friendly models.

The mildly technophobic or simply non-technical are often baffled and bewildered by the range and quality of new equipment they are offered. High-tech equipment, once the preserve of the rich or simply dotty, is everywhere: in the kitchen, the bedroom, the car and certainly the office. The British, we are told, are highly creative and inventive, but our scientists are not interested in or able to translate these new ideas into commercial products. Paradoxically, international comparisons show that despite their love of tradition and natural conservatism, the British are relatively quick on the uptake in respect of new technology.

But what determines the uptake of innovations? Which type of person gets in first and why, and who are those souls dragged kicking and screaming into the twentieth century? There have been attempts to distinguish between various styles of adapting to change or being creative. Thus we have those more conforming and conservative types who try for well-established solutions to technical problems. Their creativity as such is aimed at doing things better. There are, however, others who prefer to try to do things differently – to define the problem and its solution in completely novel ways. The former prefer gradual, adaptive, step-by-step change, the latter dramatic, highly innovative and very 'alternative' solutions. This is not to mention those who refuse to come to terms with the necessity for change at all!

More importantly, how do manufacturers or legislators encourage technology uptake? How do they encourage the reticent on the one hand but also satisfy the thirst for new products on the other?

We all know about the S-shaped learning curve. The diffusion curve is much the same. That is, initial uptake is slow and done only by a few. Then there is a noticeable, fast, steep increase as the idea or product takes off. The curve flattens again when the market becomes saturated or the idea 'old hat'. And it seems to contain five clear types of individuals. The first are the *Innovators*. These are individuals who are always seeking to innovate or try out new ideas or equipment. They come in many shapes or forms: the 'Clive Sinclair' eccentric, innovating genius; the child-like adult who, deprived of a train set in his childhood has been compensating ever since; the socially inadequate technophile who prefers electricity to interaction. They may scour the pages of specialist magazines for new equipment or may even try building it themselves. They had CDs, computers, microwaves and faxes long before most people even knew what they were. Some can be innovation junkies who go for anything new and different irrespective of its quality, usefulness or design. Others like to improve on current ideas and techniques.

The next group are the *Early Adopters*. These people take little or no persuasion and are among the first of the populus to take on the innovation. They are at the beginning of the steep climb of the S curve. All they have to be told is that there is new equipment which is faster, smarter or more elegant than theirs, and they want it. This applies not only to technology but to more abstract concepts such as ideas and behaviour patterns. Early adopters gave up smoking and took up muesli before most others and knew the importance of politically correct language – ideal types for the advertiser or legislator because one mention of the product is sufficient to spur them to buy.

As the diffusion of innovation occurs and the new phenomenon becomes recognised, the *Early Majority* begin to take an interest. They need to be sold the idea; persuaded to buy. A little sceptical and a little cautious, the early majority are good candidates to adopt innovation, but need some convincing. This is the mid-point on the diffusion curve and includes the bulk of the population. The product or the idea appears in the media and in shops more widely than before and the new 'thing' appears to be everywhere.

The *Late Majority* need the hard sell. Scepticism turns to cynicism when they are faced with an innovation and they frequently demand that its benefits are proved to them. Like all of us, they have probably bought some new idea or product which proved to be pretty useless or unreliable and have not forgotten it. For them, the cupboard of unused gizmos – the toasted sandwich maker, the slow cooker, the exercise bicycle – is an unwelcome reminder of previous purchasing imprudence. Some argue that the later one adopts an innovation, the cheaper it is and the more reliable. The pocket calculator is one example among many and this also persuades the late majority to be cautious; perhaps rather too cautious for the advertiser.

Finally, at the top of the curve is the *Laggard*. Like innovators, laggards come in very different forms but share a common reaction to innovation. There is the technophobe, simply petrified of anything not simple and mechanical. There is the young fogey who rejoices in the quill pen over the computer. There is the change averse who hates learning anything new. They all share a fear of and hostility to innovation. For employers and legislators, the only way to make them comply is to change the rules. You have to ban or physically remove old equipment, or make laws (for instance about seat belts or gas appliances) to achieve compliance. There are few easy ways to persuade the laggard, and advertising of product benefits is a waste of time for this group.

The problem of the diffusion of innovation for the manufacturer is threefold. First they have to segment their market and be able to identify the demographic, geographic and psychographic correlates of the five different types mentioned above. Next they have to either change their marketing strategy as the population moves up the S curve or target it quite specifically to the different groups. But the third problem is greatest of all: what to do when even the laggards have adopted the innovation. The only solution is to find a new product, a new idea, a new approach and start all over again. And, of course, manufacturers, like their customers, can also be classified by the same fivefold scheme as described above.

In the workplace, too, managers might benefit by understanding the attitudes to innovation of their workforce and adapting training programmes accordingly. Easy enough for the innovators who probably already demand innovation from their company, but it has to be the rule book and the big stick for the laggards.

12. You Can't Learn Anything from Case Studies of Other Companies

Organisations, like individuals, have one thing in common: they are all different. Each company is unique even if its products are not. If this is true why do students of business try to learn from case studies? Can one understand general principles by looking at unique examples?

Are case histories anything more than amusing and interesting stories of business success and failure? Or are they the Aesop's fables of the twentieth century?

Business gurus and textbook authors have realised the appeal of the case history study. Storming up and down the stage with the zeal and zealotry of evangelical preachers, many (American) business gurus such as Tom Peters tell heart-rending stories of how often, by stunningly simple changes, whole organisations were rescued from certain bankruptcy and their employees saved from redundancy. Less attractive, perhaps, are those smug autobiographies by million-aire megalomaniacs who tell their own stories of 'tea-boy to manag-ing director' fame. Many best-selling business books are simply a catalogue of interesting and unusual case histories that nicely illus-trate some point or other. Even business textbooks often illustrate points by describing, in neat boxes, personal case histories.

For hard scientists, and even for the despised and oxymoronic social scientists, the idea of teaching by parable is bizarre. Does management science have no facts, formulae or theories which can, and should, be taught by the conventional methods? The axioms of physics and maths are set and agreed and everything in the subject based on them. But management science either has no axioms or else they are constantly changing. And how does one examine the learning derived from parable-like case histories?

Indeed, case histories are remarkably like parables – they are our modern moral tales. The prodigal son's return, the good Samaritan who crossed the street, and the investor of the three talents all have their modern equivalents.

So why teach by parable? Advocates of the system argue that there are quite specific benefits. First, the case histories are *realistic* and usually highly *relevant*. They are not abstract examples with foreign jargon. It is easy for students to identify with these everyday examples from that familiar place called the real world. Often they are based on actual happenings – only the names are changed to avoid litigation.

Second, these stories are highly *memorable*. It is often the little and amusing frills that make the story unforgettable, even after a lengthy period of time. Of course, one may not always recall the most salient aspect of the case and remember only some ephemeral embellish-ment, but stories stick better than formulae.

Third, and perhaps paradoxically, the case-study parables have different interpretations. Just as biblical parables have kept theolo-gians busy for two millennia trying to puzzle out the exact meaning of the stories, so the ambiguities in the case study make it ripe for multiple interpretations. This suggests that as a learning tool it encourages *participation* by raising different viewpoints. Alternative insights, solutions or implications can easily be extracted, evaluated and debated. The very rich *complexity* of the case study makes it very difficult to analyse exhaustively, and in this sense mirrors the real business problems which the students will confront later in their careers.

Finally, the case-study students not only have to generate different interpretations, but they have to argue and *compete* for their perspective. Thus, case-study interpretation encourages *mental flexibility*, and the ability to *marshal evidence* in favour of a particular explanation.

Critics of the case-study approach see management (science) as having no facts or theories. But what they forget is that medical students – for better or worse – use case studies for all of the above reasons. Indeed, one could argue that lawyers are educated exclusively through the case study. Businessmen, like lawyers, are encouraged to draw abstract principles from specific case histories.

Of course a good case study is as rare as a good parable. Hence the vigilance of business academics for a good case to enrich their bible of examples. Boys scouts learned manliness and fieldcraft by telling ripping yarns around the campfire. Businessmen may do the same by recounting a personal experience in the bar. Bear this educational principle in mind next time you join a late-night huddle at a business conference!

13. Most Management Training Works

Most big organisations attempt to provide some sort of training for their managers, either in-house or bought in. Always done with good intention, it can be both extremely expensive and conspicuously ineffective. Very frequently, the people who plan or pay for the training are disappointed because the results are not what they expected or hoped for. Is this because their expectations are inappropriate, their training methods flawed, or their managers untrainable?

The first problem lies in determining the goals of management training. These may be general or specific; implicit or explicit; realistic or unrealistic; achievable or impossible; measurable or simply determined by gut feel; trackable or not. Most management training is about the acquisition of some skill – technical or interpersonal – though it could also be about insight and increasing sensitivity. As such, management training is frequently, but certainly not always, modestly successful. The question, however, remains why the skill is not retained between the classroom and the office.

Apart from skill acquisition, management training can offer other serendipitous benefits. Courses allow people from different parts of the organisation to network, to compare and contrast and to establish lateral links. It may be an expensive way of bringing people together but it can be very effective, particularly if trainees are required to operate on the course in competitive teams or undergo outward-bound-type dangers.

Courses can also help to change the culture of an organisation, either deliberately or not. Taught similar skills, or even concepts/terms, employees develop into a more homogeneous body who, despite the fact that they have different functions and expertise, seek a common language.

Some management training courses may also be perceived as a perk for attendees, not because they represent time away from the daily grind, but rather because they permit the acquisition of some highly useful, valuable and transportable skills. In this sense, management training facilitates career development and may be seen by employees as a positive plus.

But most organisations have a training department, or hire in training consultants, in order to make their staff more efficient and effective. A laudable aim but frequently unfulfilled. Why? The following are some of the reasons why many management training courses fail to deliver enough bang for the (frequently large) bucks.

Training programmes 'fail' for the following reasons. These may be used as a checklist to prevent wasting money.

1. *Lack of training is the wrong diagnosis.* Training is the answer to poor or no education. It is not the answer to poor motivation, bad management or someone with no ability. No training course can help morale in the long run. Too frequently, training is seen as the panacea for structural or morale issues and thus must fail.

2. *The training outcome is not specified.* It often happens that there is little or no specified outcome for the course. If neither the trainer nor the participant is able to specify an explicit set of desired outcomes it can never be known whether the course has failed or not.

3. *The training outcome expectations are unrealistic.* How long does it take to become a competent second-language speaker, or a 70-word-a-minute typist? The answer is nearly always longer

than you think. Higher-level skills are not that easily acquired and take time to master. Naively optimistic managers expect too much of a short training course and such high expectations cannot be fulfilled.

4. *Training is not of the right type.* There are many types of training such as experiential, instructional and self-paced learning. Some training concerns theoretical ideas, some concerns practice. Not all skills are best taught in the same way. Language skills, management skills and computer skills may require rather different training methods. The preferences of the trainer and the trainee combined with the skill being taught should mean that the appropriate method is being used.

5. *The training course is too short.* New skills need to be practised and if financial constraints mean that the course is too short there is quite clearly insufficient opportunity to learn. In fact, it is better to have a few short courses distributed over time in order to provide the opportunity of practising the skill in the real world. In psychobabble, distributed is better than massed learning.

6. *Training goals are not related to work goals.* Unless the trainee and the manager have got together and made sure they agree on the ultimate goals of the training it is quite possible that one or other will be disappointed. It is surprisingly rare for the two parties to discuss explicitly what they want.

7. *New skills are not supported by the environment.* When a trainee returns to the workplace, he or she needs to practise the new skills learnt, otherwise they soon fall into decay. New skills may require new technology and certainly require new styles of supervision. Frequently, however, jealous and incompetent managers punish, rather than reward, new skills and hence extinguish the beneficial effects of training.

8. *There is no accountability for follow-up or implementation.* If nobody is given the responsibility for ensuring that the training works – i.e. that it is measured – it is not surprising that new skills slip into disuse. It is not only the responsibility of the trainee to practise, maintain and even improve on the newly acquired skills. It is also the responsibility, or should be, of those who initiated the training to make sure that expensively acquired skills are duly used.

If you think training is expensive, try ignorance and lack of skill. But training has to be carefully planned and thought through. It does not have to be expensive, but it does have to be continuous. The KAIZEN principle of continuous improvement in fact suggests that training is not something one has at the beginning of a career or new job, occasionally topped up by periodic courses. Training to be better is a lifelong activity, not a quick fix.

Training programmes can be a bottomless pit for those keen on throwing money at the problem.

Using high-trust, low-threat 'learning environments', many middle-management courses focus on personal renewal and the development of skills. These courses play an important (even life-changing) role in their participants' personal and professional lives. Then a typical scenario emerges. After the course the participants return to their organisation. Because no one else from the organisation was on the course the ex-participant gets little reward for his/her experience. Any notions about change and new ideas are knocked out of their minds by the daily tasks and problems. As a result many course participants report that they are more frustrated by their inability to affect the organisation than they were before they attended the course!

Training courses work in the sense that learning occurs and is retained under specific conditions. People must want to learn and attend the course: one volunteer is worth ten conscripts. People need reinforcement and rewards for skill acquisition, not to be ignored, despised or punished. Practice of skills is imperative and needs to be distributed over time.

Personnel magazines are full of residential training course advertisements. They promise the earth and a fully changed individual – motivated, insightful, skilled, enthusiastic. Often the person who returns after a training course is exhausted, over-fed and a bit bewildered. Training courses can change people's lives but not always in ways anticipated by those well-meaning employers who sponsor them.

Chapter 3:
Myths about
Decision Making

- Nothing recedes like success (Walter Winchell).
- You must believe the unbelievable, snatch the possible out of the impossible (Don King).
- Meetings are indispensable when you don't want to do anything (Kenneth Galbraith).
- Persuade the decision takers that the decision you want is their idea (Michael Shea).
- All decisions should be made as low as possible in the organisation. The Charge of the Light Brigade was ordered by an officer who wasn't there looking at the territory (Robert Townsend).

The ability to take wise timely decisions *and* to act upon them is central to good management. Decision making is both a creative and an analytical task. To arrive at a good decision managers need to be able to consider the full range of alternatives. Bad decisions may simply be the result of not fully considering all the different (radical, unusual) alternatives. Many great innovative ideas are the result of lateral thinking and trying out quite different methods.

Some decisions in fact have to be creative. The worlds of advertising, public relations and to some extent research require the decision maker to come up with new ideas. But how is this best done: pondering the problem alone (while walking, having a bath); discussing it casually with friends; or brainstorming in groups? Brainstorming is very popular but it can be much less efficient than pooling the ideas of individuals working alone. Usually brainstorming is used when it is least effective.

So why are so many decisions made (or avoided) in groups? The answer is essentially twofold: first there is diffusion of responsibility which is particularly salient if the decision is important and it could go wrong. No one individual but all of those committed are to blame. Second, being part of a decision-making group (team, committee) means that one can have one's say in the final decision. And this participation usually leads to ownership in the sense that people are more likely to abide by, accept and enforce decisions in which they have participated.

But committees are also places where decisions can be avoided. The skilled committee person knows all the tricks not of making decisions in committee but rather avoiding them!

The search for the best decision-making strategy, like the quest for a successful change-orientation strategy, is not unlike the search for the Holy Grail...long lasting, but doomed to failure. There are a number of different strategies, each with advantages and limitations. These may be used by different organisations, at different times, with varying success.

Whilst it may be frowned upon at school, copying from others is no sin in the world of business. If someone has a good idea, an excellent product or a successful process, copy it. The Japanese are famous for taking ideas from others and copying them but improving upon them. But we have learnt to copy from them also. Cultures have quite different deeply ingrained assumptions about who, how, when and where decisions are made. It is by studying others that we can best reflect upon ourselves.

Finally, decision making usually calls for honesty, something of a sparse commodity on the battlefield of the board room. Can one detect those telling the truth? There are tell-tale non-verbal signs of lying but what about the response to questionnaires? Can we catch the liar on simple attitude questionnaires? The answer is yes – more easily than perhaps you believe.

14. Brainstorming is the Best Way to be Creative in Groups

Can creativity be taught? How do we come up with a really innovative idea? What is the best method for generating ideas? For many, the answer to these problems is brainstorming. The dictionary definition of a brainstorm is, curiously, 'temporary mental upset marked by uncontrolled emotion and violent action'. But does it work to solve problems or come up with new ideas?

Brainstorming is used most frequently to generate as many solutions to a particular problem as possible because quantity is favoured over quality. The product of a brainstorming session is ideally a wide range of possible conclusions (options, solutions) which can be presented to a third party qualified to pick the best one. The basic assumption is that 'two heads are better than one' and that together, in groups, innovative solutions can be found. But does brainstorming work? It can, but only under very special circumstances! The technique or rules of brainstorming are quite simple. The first is *free-wheeling*. Participants are encouraged to be different, to break the mould, to let rip and allow any crazy idea or association into the solution. Silence is discouraged and nothing is unacceptable.

The second rule is *no criticism*. In order to encourage the wild ideas the participants should not be put off by the disapproval of others. At this stage all ideas, however way out (indeed because they are unusual), are equally valuable.

The third rule is that *piggy-backing is OK*. This means that it is quite acceptable to jump on the back of others; to run with their ideas and to follow someone down an unusual path. Indeed this is precisely why this activity is group-oriented. Groups supposedly give one synergy and energy, and provide stimulation. But do they? In all circumstances? One very important factor in whether decisions are better made by groups or by individuals rests on one of the characteristics of the problem: how well structured or poorly structured is the issue about which decision is to be made?

Imagine working on a problem that requires several very specific steps and has a definite right or wrong answer, such as an arithmetic problem or a crossword puzzle. How can one expect to perform on such a *well-structured* task when working alone compared with when working with a group of people? Research findings indicate that groups performing well-structured tasks tend to make better, more accurate decisions, but take more time to reach them than individuals. In one study, people worked either alone or in groups of five on several well-structured problems. Comparisons between groups and individuals were made with respect to accuracy (the number of problems solved correctly) and speed (the time it took to solve the problems). It was found that the average accuracy of groups of five persons working together was greater than the average accuracy of five individuals working alone. However, it was also found that groups were substantially slower (as much as 40%) than individuals in reaching solutions.

There are essentially three reasons why decision making, or idea generating, in groups doesn't work. They are, in the jargon of psychology:

1.   *Social Loafing* – where an individual contribution is not (rather than cannot) be measured, some people tend to do little or nothing, relying on other, more conscientious team members.
2.   *Evaluation Apprehension* – because people in a brainstorming group are of different status, experience and reputation some feel apprehensive about their contribution being evaluated. In short no one wants to appear to be a fool...so he/she either says nothing or presents a less radical view.
3.   *Production Blocking* – because it is difficult to think and impossible to speak when somebody else is, people have to wait their turn and hence waste time. Individual production is often blocked by garrulous and vacuous others speaking.

Groups are accurate but slow. The potential advantage that groups might enjoy is being able to pool their resources and combine their knowledge to generate a wide variety of approaches to problems. For these benefits to be realised, however, it is essential that the group members have the necessary knowledge and skills to contribute to the group's task. In short, for there to be a beneficial effect of pooling of resources, there has to be something to pool. Two heads may be better than one only when neither is a blockhead: the 'pooling of ignorance' does not help at all.

But most of the problems faced by organisations are *not* well structured. They do not have any obvious steps or parts, and there is no obviously right or wrong answer. Such problems are referred to as *poorly structured*. Creative thinking is required to make decisions on poorly structured tasks. For example, a company deciding how to use a newly developed chemical in its consumer products is facing a poorly structured task. Other poorly structured tasks include: coming up with a new product name, image or logo; or finding new or original uses for familiar objects such as a coat-hanger, paper clip or brick. Although you may expect that the complexity of such creative problems would give groups a natural advantage, this is *not* the case. In fact, research has shown that on poorly structured, creative tasks, individuals perform better than groups. Specifically, in one study people were given 35 minutes to consider the consequences of everybody suddenly going blind. Comparisons were made of the number of ideas/issues/outcomes generated by groups of four or seven people and a like number of individuals working on the same problem alone. Individuals were far more productive than groups and arrived at their answers much faster.

Thus what the research seems to indicate is the opposite of what many believe. Most brainstorming is used by creative organisations which care little about the skill composition of the problem-solving groups who are then confronted with poorly structured tasks such as thinking of the name for a new product. In other words, brainstorming is used when it is *least* effective, and rarely when it is *most* effective.

How does brainstorming translate into other languages? For a non-native speaker it may be associated linguistically with an epileptic fit or a splitting headache. Certainly, for some people the experience of taking part in this activity to solve a creative, open-ended task leads to a migraine. The paradox of brainstorming is that this technique is most frequently used when research suggests it is least effective.

15. It's Difficult Avoiding Important Work Decisions

Having constantly to make important decisions causes considerable stress. Psychologists in the 1960s made monkeys develop stomach ulcers and other signs of corporate stress simply by forcing them to make decisions. In the now notorious 'executive monkey' studies, otherwise carefree animals had to choose between options with significant physical consequences such as electric shock, and the consistent monitoring and worrying led them to become ill.

And so it is with the modern manager. Told constantly about the importance of change, development, customer satisfaction etc., many middle and senior managers long for a period of stability or, as the Prayer Book has it, 'eternal changelessness'.

The stress of making decisions naturally leads to the development of numerous effective decision-avoidance techniques. Without doubt, the most popular is to appoint a committee to help the delaying tactics. Essentially, the logic of decision making goes like this: if you can avoid a decision, do so and if you can't, delay it; if you can get somebody else to avoid a decision, don't do the avoiding yourself; but if you can't avoid it, get a colleague to appoint a committee.

A good decision-avoidance committee is a group of people who individually prefer to do nothing and who collectively can meet and decide that nothing can be done. Furthermore the possibility of avoiding a decision increases in proportion to the square of the number of members of the committee.

Committee behaviour positively facilitates decision avoidance. Thus, as Parkinson observed, the time spent on any item on the agenda is inversely proportional to the sum of money involved. Also, committees handle trivial matters promptly; the important issues are delayed and rarely solved. But from the delay perspective there is always one sure result: if a committee meets over a long enough period of time, the meetings become more important than the problem they were intended to solve.

People are unused to thinking in groups – they talk, argue, adjudicate, compromise, joke, even sleep in groups – but they do not think. In consequence, a really new creative idea tends to destabilise groups and upset consensus. The committee is thus a group which is impelled to agree and is instinctively hostile to that which is divisive or new.

Failing the decision-by-committee avoidance tactic, individuals can resort to their own preferred approach. These avoidance techniques can be used by the same individuals in different situations with equal effectiveness, depending on the type and consequences of the decision and personality of the decision taker. Probably the six most favoured methods of avoiding a decision when one is requested are:

- *The temper-tantrum method:* Here the decision avoider regresses to the behaviour pattern of a spoilt two-year-old: call the decision requester names, stamp the foot, appear outraged or insulted or even apoplectic. If possible weep with indignation. Often the surprised and embarrassed requester will immediately step down.

- *The hush-hush method:* Call the requester to one side, and in a conspiratorial stage whisper, point out that he/she is rushing in where angels fear to tread. Suggest that they clearly don't understand the latest company figures, the real wishes of the CEO, the contents of the secret corporate plan etc., and that requesting such a decision will make them look naive, even idiotic. Threatened with this sort of career-limiting move, most decision requesters will back off.

- *The clarification method:* This is the 'more details please' approach. The person requesting a decision is asked to provide more specifically the reason for, and the nature and consequences of, the possible options available. This analysis –paralysis method is aimed at exhausting the decision requester as a fisherman exhausts a great marlin at the end of a line. The request for clarification is, of course, potentially endless and has nothing to do with actually gaining information. Most requesters eventually give up and thus no decision is made.

- *The double-talk method*: This method is favoured by those with a command of consultant psychobabble or consultant-speak. The use of management jargon can easily confuse those not fully conversant in this ambiguous language. Try: 'But that's against the delayering, re-engineering ethos of this company' or 'How does that square with empowerment quality circles?'. The aim is to confuse the requester and it often works.

- *The denial method*: Delay is the deadliest form of denial but also the most primitive. Denying that a decision has to be made and that a situation requires change can be very effective. Said with the square jaw of 'they shall not pass', the denial technique, if consistent and strongly 'nyet'-sounding, has been known to be highly effective.

- *The 'that's your problem shorty' method*: This method is to hand the problem straight back to the requester. The idea is to make them feel weak, selfish, even demanding, but this requires skill in developing the appropriate degree of hauteur. Handing the problem back to the requester needs to make them feel they should either be adapting to the current situation or making the decision for themselves.

- *The 'haven't got time/tear jerker' method*: Here, the decision maker will state plainly that he/she hasn't got time to consider the problem, but cleverly manages to come up with a reason which makes the requester feel a schmuck. For example: 'The CEO has just asked for a report. I'm probably going to have to work the whole weekend as it is.' Absence or resignation of a key member of staff also works as an excuse Failing any internal excuse, a close relation just admitted to intensive care is usually a winner.

- *The 'pass the buck' method*: For example: 'Do ask John, he has the latest figures' or 'That will have to go before the board. Pity you've just missed the last meeting, the next one is in a couple of months.'

- *The 'I'm glad you called' method*: This is followed by a swift change of subject, ending with the requester being given something to investigate. The decision maker should speak quickly and, where fitting, should turn down his/her hearing aid. It works best on the telephone so the persistent requester can be cut off with 'I must go, John's just arrived for a meeting', or, as a last resort, a telephone malfunction.

Other techniques involve calling in consultants, the most expensive form of delay, or cultivating the reputation of being an Abominable No-Man.

Some might side with Victor Kiam, who noted that 'Procrastination is opportunity's natural assassin'. However, decision avoiders are more likely to believe Thurber's 'He who hesitates is often saved'. But don't procrastinate – learn a decision-avoidance technique today.

16. There is Only One Good Way to Introduce Organisational Change

The trouble with both the idea and practice of organisational change is that it is, at the same time, both dull and anxiety provoking. The number of magazine and newspaper articles, courses, memos and self-help books – all dealing with the need for change – is overwhelming and overwhelmingly boring as a result.

But the idea of change and learning to adapt, at any age, is stressful. Learning new skills, or how to treat staff and customers differently, or how to face the ruthlessness of market forces naturally induces anxiety.

It also causes problems for those who have to, or choose to bring about change. 'Adapt or die: change or decay' is not a simple rallying cry for the senior manager. It is a reality. The question is how to bring about successful change to maximise effectiveness and minimise pain.

Managers choose different strategies with very different consequences.

1.   *The Fellowship Strategy*: This approach relies heavily on interpersonal relations and hence uses seminars, dinners and events to announce and discuss what needs to be changed and how. People at all levels are listened to, supposedly treated equally and conflicting opinions are expressed. This 'warm and fuzzy' approach emphasises personal commitment over ideas and the change process may have serious problems getting going as a consequence. But being conflict-averse, this strategy actually ducks crucial issues and flounders; it even wastes time conspicuously. In the end, many non-fellowship types leave the organisation out of frustration and can only be replaced by those people who have a need to belong.

2.   *The Political Strategy*: This approach targets the power structure by attempting to influence the official and unofficial leaders. The strategy seeks to identify and persuade those in the organ-

isation who are most respected and who have large constituencies. Political strategists flatter, bargain and compromise to achieve their ends. But this strategy destabilises the organisation because of the ongoing shift in people's political stances. It can also have problems maintaining credibility because it is so obviously devious, and managers who choose this approach often have great difficulty with questions of values, ethics and loyalty, given all the resulting conspiracies. Getting people to show their true colours through this strategy is never simple

3.   *The Economic Strategy*: The cynical economist believes that money is the best persuader. The person who controls the purse strings can buy or change anything. Everybody has their price. This is the rational 'homo economicus' approach which assumes that people act more or less logically, but that their logic is based on economic motives. However, 'buying people off' can be both costly and too dependent on economic motives, and also short-term. People adapt to money changes too fast for them to be truly effective in the long term. This strategy also suppresses and ignores all questions that are not answerable in bottom-line profit or loss terms. Also, of course, all emotional issues are ignored.

4.   *The Academic Strategy*: This approach assumes that if you present people with enough information and the correct facts they will accept the need to change and will actually do so. The academic strategist commissions studies and reports, with employees, experts and consultants to do the research. They value the detached, disinterested, analytic approach. Although these strategists are happy to share their findings, it is extremely difficult, after the analysis phase, to mobilise energy and resources to do anything. Analysis paralysis often results because the study phase lasts too long. So long, in fact, that the results and recommendations are often out of date when they are published. Cynics also suggest the consultants are paid by the weight of their reports, not by the effectiveness of their contribution!

5.   *The Engineering Strategy*: This is the technocratic approach which assumes that if the physical nature of the job is changed (by using new equipment in a different layout) enough people will be forced to change. The strong emphasis on the structural aspects of problems leads to a sensitivity to the working environment, which is particularly helpful in unstable situations. The concern with channels of communication is also helpful.

The trouble is, most people don't like being treated as machines, and hence do not feel committed to changes. Structural or environmental change can produce unexpected results by breaking up happy and efficient teams. Finally, this approach is limited because only really high-level managers can conceive what it is all about. The approach is far too impersonal and ignores the most important question for all those being changed: what is in this for me?

6. *The Military Strategy*: This approach, reliant on brute force and sometimes ignorance, is not the exclusive preserve of the military or paramilitary organisations such as the police, but also of radical groups such as anti-hunt demonstrators, animal rights groups and extremist political parties. The stress is on learning to use the weapons for the fight. Physical strength, agility and scrupulous following of the plan are rewarded. The discipline of the military approach excels when the maintenance of order is required. But a drawback of this strategy is that the change enforcer can never relax, otherwise the imposed change will disappear. Furthermore, force is met by force and the result is an ever-escalating cycle of violence. Change, yes, but not the desired change at all.

7. *The Confrontational Strategy:* This high-risk emotional strategy reckons that if you can arouse and then mobilise anger in people to confront a problem, they will change as a result. Much depends on the strategists' ability to argue the points, as well as direct and control the stirred-up anger without resorting to violence. This approach even encourages people to confront problems they would prefer not to address and to bring things out into the open. However, all this realised anger tends to focus too much on the problem and not on the solution. Anger and conflict also tend to polarise people and can cause a major backlash. The British, in particular, find this approach to change, with its display of highly charged emotions, extremely uncomfortable.

Of course, few of these strategies occur in pure form. But they do each have quite different basic assumptions about who to influence, how to proceed, and what to focus on. Each tends to be good for certain change problems but seriously bad for others. Thus the political strategy has problems with credibility, the economic approach with maintaining change, and the academic with implementing findings. However for forward-thinking HR professionals who must demonstrate their worth to the organisation by implementing change, any of the above might well help them 'contribute to the commercial success of the business'.

The trouble is that some strategies rather than others tend to be favoured by CEOs for personal reasons. The main change agent's personality, pathology and purse strings seem to determine the strategy rather than any well-considered set of options. Thus, to choose and implement an inappropriate strategy in a partisan and insensitive way may cause more trouble than the reason for change itself.

17. We Have Nothing to Learn from the Japanese

Fifteen years ago the management guru William Ouchi tried to explain to increasingly envious and paranoid Americans and Europeans the cause of Japanese manufacturing success. What accounts for Japanese quality, productivity, industrial relations and export success?

1. *Lifetime employment:* Employees in many (but by no means all) Japanese companies are virtually assured a position for life. Feeling that their future is intimately linked with that of their company, they become deeply committed to it and unwilling to strike.
2. *Slow evaluation and promotion:* Evaluation and promotion are both relatively slow in most Japanese companies. Thus, an individual's performance can be appraised by many persons over a period of several years. This leads employees to realise that the company has a 'memory' and will ultimately reward faithful service. It also instils great confidence that their performance will be fairly and accurately evaluated.
3. *Non-specialised career paths:* Many employees in Japanese companies – especially those at high levels – perform several different jobs during their careers. This leads to lessened commitment or identification with their own occupation or field, and to greater involvement in the company. This reduces departmental squabbles.
4. *Consensual decision making:* Decisions in most Japanese companies are made collectively, through a process in which all persons affected have a chance to provide input. This strengthens feelings of involvement within the organisation because it is easier to own a decision when you have taken part in it.
5. *Collective responsibility:* Responsibility for success and failure is

spread among all members of a work unit or department. As each person's fate is intimately linked with that of many others, feelings of general commitment are enhanced.

6. *Holistic concern for employees.* Finally, Japanese companies are not simply interested in their employees during working hours and in work contexts. Rather, they show concern for their welfare off the job. Such concern fosters a high degree of intimacy between employees and enhances involvement with the organisation.

These patterns and preferences were, and for the most part remain, quite different from our pattern. In the West, evaluation and promotion tend to occur rapidly. Decision making and responsibility are largely individual matters. Career paths are highly specialised and there is segmented concern – the organisation is interested in employees only within the scope of company business.

But things are changing. The Japanese have experienced a major recession. The Americans have restructured and slimmed down through 'rightsizing' and have done their re-engineering. The most obvious problem for the Japanese is how to manage the lifetime employment promise in a period of recession. First it must be acknowledged that only 30% of reasonable-sized Japanese companies had lifetime guarantees. And because compulsory lay-offs lead to declining morale, recruitment problems and stigmatisation within the business community, Japanese organisations have attempted classic 'solutions'. These include voluntary retirement with attractive packages as well as promotion to the presidency of a minor subsidiary.

The slow promotion and non-specialised career path remain. The cream of the cream go into government departments such as the Ministry of Finance.

Certainly what seems to characterise so much of Japanese industry is consensus and strong strategic alliances. There is an 'iron triangle' of cooperation and respect between bureaucrats, industry and politicians. Even company shareholders are stable and friendly. Middle managers, that decimated breed in the West, play an important facilitative and communicative role. Communication in big Japanese companies is neither top down, nor bottom up. The middle manager communicates what is and what ought to be both explicitly and implicitly.

The problem, or one of them, facing Japan is that their operational efficiency is near its ceiling. Where do you go after that? Further, the competitors have stolen and copied many of the good management ideas such as 'quality circles' and 'just-in-time' management.

Many myths abound in respect of Japanese success, such as joint R&D; benevolent (indeed protectionist) government regulation; a superhuman work ethic. Japan has never been especially committed to Asia and their imperial adventures 50 years ago are still not forgotten.

The Japanese, in order to maintain their position, have had to do some rethinking. Outsourcing is much more common. Their ultimate strategy remains shrouded in secrecy. Strategic thinking is long term and the Japanese are good at that. But whilst their products and processes continually evolve, their basic management philosophy stays the same.

To all intents and purposes the business world is dominated by four subcivilisations: the Saxon, Teutonic, Gallic and Nipponese. And, partly due to the formal education and informal socialisation that every culture affords, they have rather different and diverse ways of reaching decisions. Cultural diversity is a bit of a 'flavour of the month' in management circles. Yet there is no doubt that national (and corporate) culture does have a powerful impact on business. Culture affects feelings and relationships, how we accord status, manage time and relate to nature. It also affects how we marshal evidence, present arguments and make decisions.

The *Saxon* style fosters and encourages debate and discourse. Pluralism and compromise are overriding values, and there is often the belief, particularly in America, that the individual should be built up, not put down. Accepting that there are different perspectives and convictions, the general approach is that these should be debated and openly confronted so that not only a compromise but a synthesis is produced – a sum greater than the parts. The price of ecumenism is anodyne blandness.

This is quite different in *Teutonic* and *Gallic* traditions. First, less conflict is likely to arise because groups are often more homogenous, being selected and socialised for being 'sound on the salient issues'. Teutons and Gauls love to debate, but not with antagonists, which would be considered a hopeless waste of time or an act of condescension. There is less tension-relieving humour and back slapping – the tone is stiff, formal, caustic.

The Japanese from the *Nipponese* tradition don't debate, partly through lack of experience and partly because their first rule is not to upset the pre-established social relations. They show respect for authority and collectivist solidarity. Questions are for clarification and debate is a social, rather than an intellectual act.

The British have a penchant for documentation; the Americans for statistics. Both believe that data (reality) unite and theory divides. The British are distrustful of theories and 'isms' and 'ologies': these are considered to be 'sweeping generalisations'. Reports, graphs, tables are seen as necessary back-up to support decisions.

The Germans like theories which are deductive in both senses of the word: that the theory may be deduced from other more fundamental principles and that it is fecund for practical deductions itself. It is not that they eschew data – quite the contrary – but they like to know the philosophical or economic model or theory that drives both data collection and decision making. The Gauls are impressed by the elegance of theories and approaches. The aesthetic nature of the argument is appreciated; surprising little counter-intuitions are rejoiced in. The use of *bon mots*, *double entendres*, alliterations and allusions to obscure cultural artefacts are celebrated, not shunned. For the Teutons it is rigour before elegance, but for the Gauls it is the other way round. Sometimes the sound of words is more important than their meaning.

The Nipponese might fear inconsistency, ambiguity and contradiction, but seem to be able to live with them. Arguments are less categorical and it is perfectly acceptable to see things as tentative, not fully formed. Ideas and theories are very cautiously elaborated with various kinds of excuses and apologies for their incompleteness.

In decision-making groups, the Anglo-Saxons pretend they are all equal but different; the Teutonic leaders have to pretend that they have nothing to learn; the Gauls that they are all irrelevant to one another; and the Nipponese that they all agree. Given a proposition, the Saxons question 'How can you document or measure this?'; the Teutons want to know 'How can this be deduced from first principles?'; the Gauls, of course, wonder 'Can this be expressed in French?'; whilst the Nipponese approach is to ask 'Who is the proposer's boss?'

It is no surprise therefore that courses on International Management Styles are so popular.

18. You Can't Stop People Lying in Questionnaires

Psychologists have many words for lying: dissimulation, social desirability responding and faking good. They talk of *impression management*, which means lying to make yourself look good, and of *aggrandising self-disclosure*, which means telling others untruths about oneself.

People lie for all sorts of reasons: to protect their reputation; to hide highly undesirable facts; simply to portray themselves in a better light. There are lies of omission and commission; of tactical embellishment and of erratic forgetfulness.

But for the manager as disciplinarian, as recruiter and as appraiser they are a problem. How to spot the liar; how to false-foot the dissimulator; how to tumble the bullshitter? How to know, in the decision-making committee, whether people are telling the truth?

It may be helpful to look at how psychologists attempt to catch people lying in questionnaires. Most lay people believe that the best way to catch the liar is to ask many similar (almost identical) questions and if the person responds erratically (or contradictorily) they are lying. Questionnaires often have numerous similar questions, but this is to boost their internal reliability – it has nothing to do with catching liars. But the more people believe this the better. Psychologists do it differently.

Classically there are four methods used to catch questionnaire liars, each of which may be applied face to face by the wily manager.

The first is the most simple but it is quietly effective. Tell people not to lie. Let them know you expect lies, are used to them and hence are quiet good at detecting them when they occur. Though this does not prevent exaggeration, subterfuge or selective memory, it usually serves to reduce many lies and inhibit the majority.

The second method is to have a lie scale. Consider the following questions: 'Do you always wash your hands before a meal?'; 'Have you *ever* been late for an appointment?'; 'Have you *ever* taken the credit for something someone else did?' If you answer YES, NO, NO, then, sir or madam, you are a liar. What psychologists have done is devise a series of these questions. Ask a few and see how people do. If they lie on these there is a fair chance they will lie on the others as well!

The third method is great fun in the research phase because it encourages people to lie. Prepare a set of questions and give it to three groups of people: a third are asked to 'fake good' (lie by putting themselves in a positive light); a third are asked to 'fake bad' (lie by putting themselves in a negative light) and the remainder are asked to tell the truth. What one is after is a profile of a liar. This method yields a template of the responses of the fake-good liar (and the fake-bad liar is also occasionally useful), so that one can match up the responses of the respondent with those 'known' responses of liars.

The fourth method is the old forced-choice method. People will usually not admit to negative behaviour: absenteeism-related hypochondriasis; pilfering or encouraging stock shrinkage; politicking and back-stabbing. The final way of catching the ingratiator, the liar, the cleaner-than-clean employee is to give him/her a choice. However, the method does rely on a careful and judicious assessment of the equivalence of misdeeds. Consider an example: my father said a cad was a man who peed in the bath and slept in his vest. If those two indiscretions are equal, then ask people which they are *more* likely to do/have done. It is easy to come up with these, thus 'Have you/are you more likely to (a) make a private call on company time/expenses (b) take home company stationery?'. This method forces candidates to admit the undesirable side of their behaviour.

We all know about corporate lies – we service what we sell; leave your CV and we will keep it on file; it's not the money, it's the principle but personal lying is more difficult to detect. Many contracts aren't worth the paper they are written on. One advantage of telling the truth is that you don't need a good memory for what you said happened. And the liar's punishment is not that he/she isn't believed but that, *ipso facto*, he/she cannot believe anyone else.

Chapter 4: Myths about Self-knowledge

- Wisdom is the reward you get for a lifetime of listening when you'd have preferred to talk (Douglas Larsa).
- Experience is the name everyone gives to their mistakes (Oscar Wilde).
- Fanatic: Someone who can't change his mind and won't change the subject (Winston Churchill).
- Fanaticism: Redoubling your efforts when you have forgotten your aim (George Santayana).
- The secret of business is knowing something that nobody else knows (Aristotle Onassis).
- First, make yourself a reputation for being a creative genius. Second, surround yourself with partners who are better than you are. Third, leave them to get on with it (David Ogilvy).

It is not difficult to delude oneself about one's ability, skills and knowledge. After all, we all know a colleague who without the slightest shred of evidence believes he/she has a sense of humour. And the older and more powerful we get the less we tend to receive (or accept) feedback that does not confirm our self-image.

Is management just common sense? If it is, and by definition most people have common sense, why is there so much disagreement about how to manage? And why are there so many obvious management failures? The easiest way is to test common sense assumptions against the available evidence.

Do managers know what their staff look for in a leader? Certainly there are many qualities one would look for but what are, at least from the point of view of subordinates, the most important? Determination, courage, independence? Honesty – being trustworthy, having integrity, is ranked number one! Surprised? Read on.

It is all very well dreaming about the qualities in an ideal boss, particularly when one's boss is something of a tyrant. There are people in the business world who have been rewarded for being arrogant, immoral, egocentric and uncaring. They have clawed and fought their way to the top, often at the expense of others. How does one recognise the Machiavellians and, more importantly, how does one deal with them? Not easy, but it is possible.

The major job of any manager is getting the best out of his/her staff: not easy if they have little talent – or are completely unmotivated. But even the most able and dedicated staff run into personal problems that require counselling rather than cajoling. Counselling is a skill that can be learnt. Some people are naturals. Others have to learn. Some managers don't distinguish an interrogation from a counselling session. Others try to be amateur psychologists, interpreting all behaviours as symbolic motives. Counselling skills can be assessed and taught.

The business world is one of flux; the future is unclear, even threatening. This uncertainty can be deeply threatening to some people and mildly pleasurable to others. Those happy with rule-following and who like clarity get deeply frustrated by ambiguity and tend to try to create order to compensate. Others thrive in the chaos, quite unperturbed by the uncertainty. Perhaps the two extremes cause problems to themselves and their organisations.

Finally, do workers naturally enjoy or hate work? Do they have to be forced into doing what they really hate or are they easily persuaded to give of their best? Assess your beliefs and their consequences.

19. The Art of Management is Just Common Sense

People have always been divided over whether management science is simply common sense or not. It has been described as the art of systematic oversimplification, and a management scientist as someone who would rather count than guess.

Others have seen management science as an expensive and pretentious waste of time. Furthermore, they argue that an MBA or any other form of management education is pointless unless one is in possession of common sense. Many believe it is a thousand times better to have common sense plus an expensive business school education, than to have the latter without the former. Others think that if a manager has common sense, then he/she has all the sense there is and there is nothing more worth acquiring.

However, some dons might argue that logic is one thing and common sense another. Indeed, if common sense is as unerring as calculus, as some suggest, why are so many mistakes made so often by business leaders?

Can anybody be trained to become a (good) manager or do they need some sort of native ability? For some, one pound of learning requires at least ten kilograms to apply it. Furthermore, education is only a ladder with which to gather ripe fruit from the tree of knowledge, not the fruit itself.

Cynics and biography readers are justifiably sceptical of a (university) management education. Too many really creative and successful entrepreneurs have made it without going to university. Our best managers have no MBA. It seems quite possible that the socialisation one receives at a university results in poor management insights and skills. Certainly the way universities are run leaves a lot to be desired. Nepotism, inefficiency and corruption still flourish in the groves of academe and provide a particularly poor role model for the budding manager. Why not a little quiz to determine potential management ability? Try the following simple true–false quiz.

1.	Relatively few top executives are highly competitive, aggressive and show 'time urgency'.	T/F
2.	In general, women managers show higher self-confidence than male equivalents and expect greater success in their careers.	T/F
3.	Slow learners remember more of what they learn than fast learners.	T/F
4.	To change people's behaviour towards new technology, we must first change their attitudes.	T/F
5.	The more highly motivated you are, the better you will be at solving a complex problem.	T/F
6.	The best way to ensure that high-quality work will persist after training is to reward behaviour every time, rather than intermittently, when it occurs during training.	T/F
7.	An English-speaking person with German ancestors/ relations finds it easier to learn German than an English-speaking person with French ancestors.	T/F

8. People who graduate in the upper third of the A level table tend to make more money during their careers than do average students. T/F

9. After you learn something, you forget more of it in the next few hours than in the next several days. T/F

10. People who do poorly in academic work are usually superior in mechanical ability. T/F

11. Most high-achieving managers tend to be high risk-takers. T/F

12. When people are frustrated at work they frequently become aggressive. T/F

13. Successful top managers have a greater need for money than for power. T/F

14. Women are more intuitive than men. T/F

15. Effective leaders are more concerned about people than about the task. T/F

16. Bureaucracies are inefficient and represent a bad way of running organisations. T/F

17. Unpleasant environmental conditions (crowding, loud noise, high or very low temperature) produce an immediate reduction in performance on many tasks. T/F

18. Direct, face-to-face communication usually enhances cooperation between workers. T/F

19. Women are more conforming and open to influence than men. T/F

20. Because workers resent being told what to do, giving employees specific goals interferes with their performance. T/F

1 = T 2–7 = F 8–9 = T 10–11 = F 12 = T 13–20 = F

Score 0–5   Oh dear, pretty naive or even bigoted.
Score 6–10   Too long at the school of hard knocks, we fear.
Score 11–15 Yes, experience has helped.
Score 16–20 Clearly a veteran of the management school of life.

Many people believe simple management aphorisms. A considerable number of British managers believe that, for nearly all workers, money is the most important motivating factor at work. They also believe, contrary to the evidence, that happy workers are productive workers, and that great leaders are born with the 'right type' of personality.

Education might not be the panacea for all management evils. It may not be at all helpful to people who lack some basic level of ability. It should, however, discourage people from holding simplistic, naive and even wrong views about corporate behaviour.

20. I Know What Staff Look For in a Business Leader

What are the characteristics of a good leader? Was Mao a good leader? What about Margaret Thatcher? Benito Mussolini? General Franco? Alec Douglas-Hume? Idi Amin?

Writers and researchers on the topic of leadership have tended to opt for different answers when considering the question of leadership. The 'great man' school of leadership has tried to identify great leaders and then find common characteristics which distinguish them from their followers. The 'situational leadership' school argues that leadership is context-specific, in that certain styles, abilities and attributes work only in specific situations. Thus Churchill was a great leader in wartime, but not in peacetime. The third school focuses on the behaviour of leaders who transform the situation they inherit to achieve their goals.

All these have focused on the characteristics or competencies of great leaders: leaders in politics, business, war or even big bureaucracies. They have often distilled their observations down to one or two major characteristics such as 'vision' or 'charisma'. The trouble with this approach is that it is too all-inclusive – some good leaders don't have much charisma and it does not really matter. More importantly, there are many people with a vision (or a dream) that is impractical, or unobtainable, and hence they inspire no one to follow.

The characteristics of a good leader depend considerably on your perspective. The academic writer, the leaders themselves and the followers may not all value the same characteristics. In other words, what may appear important to the manager may not be the same as the perspective of the subordinates. What followers want from their leaders, and what their leaders believe they need to demonstrate, are often two very different things.

This point was nicely illustrated by two American academics called Kouzes and Posner. First, they tried to provide a comprehensive but parsimonious catalogue of characteristics necessary for good leaders. They then assessed people in leadership or managerial roles against this list. Of course, they were not all great leaders or leaders of very big organisations. But, surprisingly perhaps, the results were quite clear. Try it out for yourself.

Characteristics of Superior Leadership

We look for some special qualities in our leaders. One recent study of managers has found that the attributes listed below account for most of the qualities we admire in our superiors at work. Review the list, then select from it five characteristics that you look for most in a leader or someone you would want to follow. Also list the five least important.

Ambitious
(hard working, aspiring)

Broad minded
(open minded, flexible, receptive)

Caring
(sensitive, appreciative, concerned, respectful, loving)

Competent
(capable, productive, effective, efficient, thorough)

Cooperative
(friendly, team player, available, responsive)

Courageous
(daring, stands up for own beliefs)

Dependable
(reliable, conscientious, responsible)

Determined
(hard working, persistent, purposeful, steadfast)

Fair-minded
(objective, forgiving, willing to pardon others, consistent)

Forward-looking
(visionary, farsighted, concerned about the future, sense of direction)

Honest
(truthful, has integrity, trustworthy, has character)

Imaginative
(creative, innovative, curious)

Independent
(self-reliant, self-sufficient, self-confident)

Inspiring
(uplifting, enthusiastic, energetic, humorous, cheerful, positive about future)

Intelligent
(bright, thoughtful, intellectual, reflective, loyal)

Loyal
(obedient, dutiful, respectful, committed to company)

Mature
(experienced, wise, has depth)

Self-controlled
(restrained, self-disciplined)

Straightforward
(direct, candid, forthright)

Supportive
(understanding, helpful)

The top five and bottom five were fairly consistently chosen. The top were: 1 honest, 2 competent, 3 forward looking, 4 inspiring and 5 intelligent. The bottom were: 16 ambitious, 17 determined, 18 self-controlled, 19 loyal and 20 independent. Traits such as imaginative, courageous and caring came pretty far down the list.

What these data say, and this type of study has been frequently repeated, is that what followers want is bright people with a 'vision thing' who give it to them straight. They don't particularly want the maverick (ambitious, independent) or the plodder (determined, self-controlled, loyal).

Good leaders do not only need to be able to do five things well. They also need to be open to innovation (to experiment, take risks, search for opportunities); to have a clear, inspired vision (of the future of the organisation, process or product); to enable and help others (fostering collaboration and support); to model the way (by setting a good example); and to 'encourage the heart' (by recognising individual contributions and celebrating accomplishment). And what their followers want from them no doubt changes from time to time, and from organisation to organisation.

Leaders have their power and influence conferred by those under them. Credibility comes upwards in the organisation. But one has to earn the leadership role by being upbeat, upfront, up to the job, up to date and being seen as up and coming. Being uppity, uptight or keen to upstage won't do.

21. I Can Deal with Machiavellians

In 1513 the Italian philosopher Niccola Machiavelli published a book entitled *The Prince*. In it, he outlined a ruthless strategy, now known as Machiavellianism, for seizing and holding political power. The main thrust of his approach was simple: other people can be readily used or manipulated by sticking to a few basic rules.

Among the guiding principles he recommended were the following: (1) never show humility – arrogance is far more effective when dealing with others; (2) morality and ethics are for the weak – powerful people feel free to lie, cheat and deceive whenever this suits their purpose; and (3) it is much better to be feared than to be loved. In general, Machiavelli urged those who desired power to adopt a totally pragmatic approach to life. Let others be swayed by considerations of friendship, loyalty, or fair play, he suggested; a truly successful leader should always be above such factors. In short, he or she should be willing to do whatever it takes to get his or her way.

That the ideas which Machiavelli proposed are still very much with us is clear – and unsettling. In fact, they are readily visible in many books which have made their way onto the bestseller lists in recent years – books which describe similar self-centred strategies for gaining power and success. The popularity of such publications suggests that people are as fascinated today by the tactics Machiavelli described as they were more than four centuries ago. But are these strategies really put to use? Are there individuals who choose to live by the ruthless, self-serving creed which Machiavelli proposed? The answer appears to be 'yes'. It is useful to know two things about 'Machs': (1) how they operate – how, precisely, they manage to manipulate others for their own gain; and (2) how you can defend yourself against them.

First, High Machs follow Machiavelli's advice about being pragmatic. As far as they are concerned, any means is justified so long as it helps them towards their goals. Thus, they are perfectly willing to lie, cheat, play 'dirty tricks', or engage in virtually any actions to succeed. Second, High Machs often possess characteristics associated with successful people including confidence, eloquence and competence. These traits, combined with their pure pragmatism, can be quite distracting. Third, High Machs are often very adept at choosing situations in which their preferred tactics are most likely to work. Such situations include those in which they can interact with the persons they intend to manipulate face to face, in which there are few clear rules, and in which others' emotions are running high. Because High Machs never let their 'hearts rule their heads' they can take full advantage of the fact that others' emotions make them especially vulnerable to manipulation. Finally, High Machs are skilled at various political manoeuvres, such as forming coalitions with others. And, as you might expect, in these coalitions most of the advantages are theirs.

Try rating yourself. Are the following statements true or false?

1. A white lie is often a good thing.   T/F

2. If one is morally right, compromise is out of the question. T/F

3. There is no point in keeping a promise if it is to your
    advantage to break it.   T/F

4. Any normal person will stand up for what he/she
    thinks is right even if it costs his/her job.   T/F

5.   Anyone who completely trusts someone else is asking
     for trouble.   T/F

6.   Some of the best people have some of the worst vices.   T/F

7.   It is safest to assume that all people have a vicious
     streak and it will come out when given a chance.   T/F

8.   One should take action only when sure it is morally
     right.   T/F

9.   Humility is not only of no service but is actually harmful. T/F

10. It is wise to flatter important people.   T/F

11. It is hard to get ahead without cutting corners here
     and there.   T/F

12. Most people don't know what is best for them.   T/F

13. Never trust anyone who has a grudge against you.   T/F

14. It is better to compromise with existing evils than to go
     out on a limb in attacking them.   T/F

15. It is safer to be feared than to be loved.   T/F

16. If a friend asks for advice, it is smart to think about
     what will happen if your advice backfires.   T/F

17. It is not a good idea to put pressure on people if
     you want them to do something.   T/F

18. Never tell anyone the real reason you did something
     unless it is useful to do so.   T/F

19. Most people are more concerned with making a
     good living than with satisfying their conscience.   T/F

20. All in all it is better to be humble and honest than to
     be important and dishonest.   T/F

Score: total number marked 'True'

Score 15–20 Have you thought of a job in the SAS?
Score 10–14 A tough guy from the school of hard knocks.
Score 6–9   A caring, honest human being.
Score 1–5   A bit idealistic and naive.

Given their lack of concern for the welfare of other people, and their
seeming lack of conscience, High Machs are wily adversaries indeed.

Yet there are strategies for protecting yourself against them. Here are several which may prove useful.

- *Expose them to others*: One reason High Machs often get away with breaking promises, lying and using 'dirty tricks' is that, in many cases, their victims choose to remain silent. This is hardly surprising: few people wish to call attention to the fact that they have been cheated or manipulated. Unfortunately, this understandable desire to protect one's ego plays directly into the High Machs' hands, leaving them free to repeat the process. One effective means of dealing with them involves exposing their unprincipled behaviour

- *Pay attention to what others do, not what they say*: High Machs are often masters at deception. They frequently succeed in convincing other people that they have their best interests at heart, just when they (the High Machs) are busy cutting the ground out from under them. Although it is often difficult to see through such machinations, focusing on what others do rather than on what they say may help. If their actions suggest that they are cold-bloodedly manipulating the people around them, even while loudly proclaiming commitment to such principles as loyalty and fair play, the chances are good that they are Machiavellian in orientation and should be carefully avoided.

- *Avoid situations that give High Machs an edge*: To ensure their success, High Machs prefer to operate in certain types of situations – ones in which others' feelings are aroused and in which others are uncertain about how to proceed. The reason for this preference is simple: High Machs realise that, under such conditions, many people will be distracted and less likely to recognise the fact that they are being manipulated for someone else's gain. It is usually wise, therefore, to avoid such situations. And if this is not possible, at least refrain from making important decisions or commitments at that time. Such restraints may make it harder for High Machs to use you for their own benefit.

22. I Know How to Counsel my Staff

The word counselling, like the word gay, has been hijacked. To counsel means simply to advise: to give professional advice through consultation.

Psychologists and social workers have so abused the word (and practice) that, except in legal circles, it has come to mean listening and mumbling platitudes while encouraging the embarrassing self-disclosure of manifold sins and wickedness which we all from time to time most grievously hath committed.

The business world, however, has recently been 'sold' the virtues of counselling. Redundancy, outplacement and career counselling are now all the rage in the personnel departments of big organisations. It is OK and not shameful to want and receive personal counselling, and the art of delivering same is now seen as a useful, indeed necessary, managerial skill. Faced with the cost and inconvenience of buying in counsellors, many organisations are attempting to acquire in-house skills by training certain HR people to become qualified and competent in general and specialist counselling duties.

All managers are frequently faced with subordinates, peers, superiors and even clients with problems which would be alleviated by a spot of good advice. But they cannot, indeed need not, all be trained in this fairly basic skill. Self-evidently, some people are better counsellors than others. The issue seems to be that individuals have preferences for, and thus adopt, particular interpersonal styles. They tend to have habitual fixed ways of dealing with others – ideal in some circumstances, hopeless in others. In the following scenarios, you are asked to imagine yourself in the role of the manager–counsellor. Pick the responses which you would be most likely to give the individual and find out your preferred counselling style:

(a) A young, well-educated female manager says: 'Two years at business school have equipped me to be a good professional manager. But competing with men has convinced me that women who get as far as I have are more than a match for most men. If this organisation wants to keep me they'll have to fit in with *my* own career progression.'

Choose one of the following responses:

1. A business school education is a great asset, but it alone doesn't make you a good manager. You have to learn that by experience.
2. What difficulties do you foresee in being female in this organisation?
3. I'm sure you're right. We are really in need of people with your ability and ambition. Let's plan out how you can get the expe-

rience you want in this department in the shortest possible time.

4. If I understand you correctly, you feel that you are a well-equipped professional manager and you expect the organisation to respect this?

5. It appears to me that you have some concerns about being accorded the status you think you deserve?

(b) A middle-aged, middle-brow, middle manager says: 'I used to be very ambitious but, as I've got older, success is less important to me. I may not have been a success with the company, but I've put all my real effort into my family. Family is probably more important to me than my job.'

Choose one of the following responses:

1. That sounds like a very sensible attitude, because very few people get to the top. Is there any help I can give you in this?

2. Yes, you reached the point where you decided to switch goals – but you feel perhaps that something is missing?

3. You're absolutely right. A man's a fool to keep struggling when nobody cares a damn. I'd do the same in your position.

4. As you have become older you have found more and more satisfaction with your family?

5. Why do you feel that you weren't a success with the company? What do you mean by success?

(c) A newly appointed manager says: 'I'm telling you X has really got his knife into me. I got the blame for the whole of the Smith & Jones affair but there were six of us involved. He's now trying to insinuate that I'm falling down on the job. I had a good reputation in this office until he came here – he just doesn't like me and he's determined to get me.'

Choose one of the following responses:

1. You are getting too paranoid about X. It could be that you are working out your frustration at not getting the job you both applied for?

2. You're right, X can be a really mean bastard when he chooses, but I wouldn't go about with your current attitude.

3. Are there any other occasions when he's tried to show you up in a poor light?

4.   If I understand you correctly, you feel hounded by X and think
      that he intends to wreck your good name?
5.   Right, you need to protect yourself from situations like this. Do
      you know that the union is becoming very strong about salary
      structure, in fact I've got some application forms here – I'll
      help you fill one out.

Scoring: tick your preferred response to each scenario	E	I	S	P	R
Statement A	1	5	3	2	4
Statement B	3	2	1	5	4
Statement C	2	1	5	3	4
No. of ticks					

The five categories of counselling styles are:
E =   Evaluation – making judgements based on available informa-
      tion.
I =   Interpretation – reading between the lines; being intuitive.
S =   Supportive – backing up and supporting people.
P =   Probing – questioning for further facts.
R =   Reflective – mirroring back or non-evaluative interpretation

Too much *probing* leads one to sound more like a litigation lawyer
than a counsellor; whilst warm, *supportive* help in excess can be
smothering. *Interpretation* without insight can be dangerous and being
reflective can be interesting but ultimately infuriating.
      The message should be clear: you need to have all these styles in
your repertoire to be a good counsellor. Most managers have a
preferred style: men are often probing; women more likely to be
supportive. The trouble with being dedicated to one style only is that
some situations call for a different style. The multiskilled multi-
talented manager knows which style to use and when.

23. I Cope Well with Uncertainty in Business

It is well known that we can be sure only of two things: death and
taxes. For the rest of life, and organisational life in particular, the
future is uncertain. Economic and political predictions are, alas,
ambiguous, mutually contradictory and frequently doom-laden.
      But it is not only the future that is unclear. All sorts of things in

our daily lives are uncertain and ambiguous. People's motives, competitor strategies, the causes of some illnesses, the behaviour of foreigners are all a mystery.

There are those who enjoy, seek out, even revel in ambiguity. They enjoy abstract art, poetry with multiple meanings, wandering in unfamiliar countries. And there are those who are made fearful and thus angry by ambiguity. They have strong needs for order, clarity, structure. They need rules, certainty and rigid dichotomisation between right and wrong. A person with a low tolerance of ambiguity experiences stress, reacts prematurely and thus avoids all sorts of ambiguous stimuli be it in art, literature, politics or emotional experience.

Those intolerant of ambiguity are not friends of change, and can be seriously out of kilter with the modern organisational world. As companies become global and multinational in terms of location, workforce and customer needs, they tend to be rather xenophobic and nationalistic. In the world of flattened, delayered structures many people long for the signs and symbols of authority in the tall hierarchical structure. Where creative lateral thinking is valued they find comfort in rule following and convergent thinking.

But before we condemn those uncomfortable with uncertainty to a 'four-legs good, two-legs bad' world, why not evaluate yourself?

1. An expert who doesn't come up with a definite answer
    probably doesn't know a great deal.   T/F

2. A good job is one where what is to be done and how it is
    to be done are clearly specified.   T/F

3. In the long run it is possible to get more done by
    tackling small, simple problems rather than larger and
    complicated ones.   T/F

4. A person who leads an even, regular life in which few
    surprises or unexpected happenings arise really has a
    lot to be grateful for.   T/F

5. I like parties where I know most of the people more than
    ones where all or most of the people are complete
    strangers.   T/F

6. The sooner we all acquire similar values and ideas the
    better.   T/F

7. People who schedule their lives all the time probably
    miss most of the joy of living.   T/F

8.   It is more fun to tackle a complicated problem than to
     solve a simple one.   T/F

9.   People who insist upon a yes or no answer just don't
     know how complicated things really are.   T/F

10. Many of our most important decisions are based upon
     insufficient information.   T/F

11. Managers who hand out vague assignments give a
     chance for subordinates to show initiative and originality. T/F

12. I have always felt that there is a clear difference
     between right and wrong.   T/F

13. Nothing gets accomplished in this world unless you
     stick to some basic rules.   T/F

14. Vague and impressionistic pictures really have little
     appeal for me.   T/F

15. Before an examination, I feel much less anxious if I
     know how many questions there will be.   T/F

16. Sometimes I rather enjoy going against the rules
     and doing things I'm not supposed to.   T/F

17. I like to fool around with new ideas, even if they turn
     out later to be a total waste of time.   T/F

18. If I were a doctor, I would prefer the uncertainties of a
     psychiatrist to the clear and definite work of a surgeon
     specialist.   T/F

19. I don't like to work on a problem unless there is a
     possibility of coming out with a clear-cut and
     unambiguous answer.   T/F

20. It bothers me when I am unable to follow another
     person's train of thought.   T/F

Scoring: The higher the score the more intolerant of ambiguity you are. Give yourself a score of 1 for each time you put T for questions 1–6, 11–15, 20. Give yourself a score of 1 for each time you put F for questions 7–10, 16–19.

Score 0–8   Perhaps an arty-farty creative.
Score 9–15   A pretty normal score and happy to recognise and
                 deal with life's little uncertainties.
Score 16–20 A conservative, call-a-spade-a-spade type.

Those who score high and don't like uncertainty usually gravitate to jobs involving technology. People are fickle, capricious and whimsical. You can't predict their behaviour very accurately; their motives are difficult to read and they change their minds. The problem lies in the fact that eventually all managers have to deal with subordinates, as well as their managers, clients and even shareholders. Those intolerant of ambiguity find this difficult and get frustrated.

The over-tolerant, with very low scores, may cause difficulties for themselves and others because, preferring not to lay down or follow rules, they don't exact high standards from their staff. They may be creative, imaginative and unusual. The moral of this story at any rate is that the middle road is the best.

24. Most Workers are Lazy, Work-shy and Feckless

A pessimist is an optimist who has had experience. Listen to the American management gurus, who seem to model both their delivery style and their beliefs on tele-evangelists, and you might believe that all workers are fundamentally good, diligent and loyal. All that is required is a corporate vision, sincerity, and a caring, ethical boss and the workforce will deliver.

The optimist, it is said, believes that we live in the best of all possible worlds and the pessimist fears this is true. Is the pessimist one who, given the choice of two evils, chooses both, or is he/she a realist? Is a pessimist one who feels bad when feeling good for fear of feeling worse when feeling better, or is he/she simply a shrewd and accurate observer of life? The British seem more reserved and sceptical than other nationalities. More used to the threat of the stick than the promise of the carrot, they appear not to hold such a rosy view of their fellow man, and less still of their fellow woman.

Followers of the French idealist Rousseau stand in sharp contrast with the bleak perception of the Englishman Thomas Hobbes. The pessimist manager might believe that 'man was born free but everywhere is in *trains*', on his way to a nasty, brutish, tedious and unsatisfying job.

For some, the experience of management is that people avoid work because they inherently dislike it. They have to be completely controlled, directed, bullied and threatened. They prefer not to shoulder responsibility or empowerment and need to be constantly monitored.

About 30 years ago an American academic called McGregor,

who was interested in what determined a person's leadership style, said that managers were likely to hold one of two 'philosophies' about workers. One, labelled THEORY X, maintained that people don't like work, avoid it, have little ambition, try to avoid responsibility and need firm direction, control and coercion. Subscribers to THEORY Y maintained that under the right conditions people not only work hard, showing commitment and talent, but also seek increased responsibility and challenge.

Test yourself to see if you are a Theory X or Y believer.

Give yourself:
4 for strongly agree
3 for agree
1 for disagree
0 for strongly disagree

Your Assumptions about People at Work:

1.	Almost everyone could probably improve his or her job performance quite a bit if he or she really wanted to.	4	3	1	0
2.	It's unrealistic to expect people to show the same enthusiasm for their work as for their favourite leisure-time activities.	4	3	1	0
3.	Even when given encouragement by the boss, very few people show the desire to improve themselves on the job.	4	3	1	0
4.	If you give people enough money, they are less likely to worry about such intangibles as status or individual recognition.	4	3	1	0
5.	Usually, when people talk about wanting more responsible jobs, they really mean they want more money and status.	4	3	1	0
6.	Being tough with people will usually get them to do what you want.	4	3	1	0
7.	Because most people don't like to make decisions on their own, it's hard to get them to assume responsibility.	4	3	1	0
8.	A good way to get people to do more work is to crack down on them once in a while.	4	3	1	0

9.   It weakens a person's prestige to admit that
      a subordinate has been right and he/she
      been wrong.   4   3   1   0

10.   The most effective supervisor is one who
      gets the results management expects,
      regardless of the methods used in handling
      people.   4   3   1   0

11.   It's too much to expect that people will try
      to do a good job without being prodded by
      the boss.   4   3   1   0

12.   The boss who expects his or her people to set
      their own standards for superior performance
      will probably find they don't set them very high. 4   3   1   0

13.   If people don't use much imagination or
      ingenuity on the job, it's probably because
      relatively few people have much of either.   4   3   1   0

14.   One problem in asking for the ideas of
      subordinates is that their perspective is too
      limited for their suggestions to be of much
      practical value.   4   3   1   0

15.   It's only human nature for people to try to do
      as little work as they can get away with.   4   3   1   0

Score under 20 and you are an optimist. You probably trust your subordinates and use a wide range of rewards. You may prefer group participation in decision making and like people to be well informed. **Score 21 to 30** and we see more caution with substantial but not complete confidence and trust in subordinates. You wish to keep control of most major decisions.
Score 31 to 45 and some may consider you a benevolent autocrat. You have a rather condescending confidence and trust, such as a master has in a servant. You tend to believe in economic motives and don't fraternise with your staff.
Score 45 and above and, let's face it, you're a cynic about the average worker. High scorers may even be exploitative autocrats who have no confidence in their subordinates, preferring physical and economic security as a motivational force. All stick and no carrot.

Top scorers despise 'soft' management techniques and maintain that the Department of Hard Knocks at the University of Life taught them what they know. Low scorers recoil in horror at the monster they see in the high scorer, equally convinced that their experience at work tells them they are right. Neither side is prepared to concede.

Hence we need the understanding to know the things we cannot change about workers; the courage to change and improve the things we can change; and the wisdom to know the difference.

Chapter 5:
Myths about
Selection

- The best executive is the one who has the sense enough to pick good men to do what he wants done, and the self-restraint to keep from meddling with them while they do it (Theodore Roosevelt).
- Work is achieved by those employees who have not reached their level of incompetence (L. Peter).
- You can only pick people you have been through the shadow of death with (Sir Bob Scholes).
- As well as a good academic record I look for people who've climbed mountains or been captain of the tiddlywinks team at university. People who other people follow (John Banham).
- If there are many applicants for a few jobs, the job is overpaid (Milton Friedman).

Choosing people through recruitment, selection and appraisal is fraught with difficulty. Each of us can probably recall making a serious error of judgement in helping to choose a person for a particular task or job.

Every individual these days is the proud possessor of a curriculum vitae, vita or résumé as the Americans prefer to call them. Supposedly they supply honestly and accurately all the relevant details of a person's life. But is this true? Aren't CVs for many people advertisements that select and distort the truth? If so, how can and should they be used in selection?

Everyone wants to be, and to be able to select, high flyers. But what are high flyers and what characteristics do they have? Clearly they need to be able – bright, trained, competent. They also need to be motivated because ability on its own will never suffice. The high flyer is able, ready and willing. But he or she needs one other quality both to be selected and to be successful at the job. It is a quality that is difficult to control and takes a great deal of nurturing.

How different are men and women at work? This is a very sensitive topic these days but we do have more and more data which allow us to shine a little light into this dark world of stereotyping and political correctness. Despite all the allegations to the contrary there are fewer differences than one may suspect.

Certainly any selector is highly sensitive to the issue of putting people together who get on and do not fight. The last thing one wants is a 'personality clash'. But what does this mean, and can it be avoided? If personality can be defined, measured and understood then surely these clashes can be predicted and explained.

The real problem in business selection is impression management – the issue that selectees carefully 'manage' the impression that they try to give in order to sell themselves to the selector. Astute interviewees are highly sensitive to fashion changes. And many know that, at least in some spheres, big is not as beautiful as it once was.

As the world shrinks and even the smallest business becomes multinational in its workforce and markets so managers are increasingly being required to live and work abroad. Some enjoy the experience so much they stay abroad or move from country to country never coming home. How easy is it to adapt to working abroad? Consider the types of expatriates we find, and see if potential managers abroad won't easily fit into the various well-known reactions.

25. A CV is an Accurate Biography

Years ago, CVs were dry, rather formal documents a bit like immigration papers. Without much attention to either presentation style or self-aggrandisement, people simply reported rather mundanely and factually the biographical details of their lives.

This rather quaint, unselfconscious approach has, in the same way as early British party political broadcasts and conferences, been taken over by the ad men, the publicity gurus, and the public relations bimbos. Politicians have learned the meaning and virtue of the sound-bite; the impression of the Italian suit versus the donkey jacket; and the benefit of the wearing the (rose) logo so that the hard-of-thinking electorate know whose side they are on. The American influence of 'talking up' nearly all personal achievements means that selectors have to be pretty subtle when reading between the lines. Likewise, ordinary people are now offered the benefits of CV consultants to improve the way they come across. No life is too ordinary, no work history too boring, no pastime too menial to be considered unworthy of the image treatment.

CV consultants are perfect strangers whose job it is to take the details of your rich, varied and complicated life and precis it into a carefully thought-out and laid-out A4 page. There are those who believe that this is really money for old rope and that they can quite happily, confidently and money-savingly do it themselves. After all, the individual knows the life history facts and the intended purpose of the CV best of all.

Psychologists call the task of CV consultants 'impression management'. It means quite simply 'attempt to change, alter and shape the impression that others receive'. Through variations in dress, vocabulary and possessions, we all try to create a favourable impression of ourselves to selected others. Given that we put in so much effort at the job interview, it makes sense to spend as much, if not more, time and money on the CV – which in itself may determine whether we ever get to the interview at all.

As a consequence of the professional treatment, the most dreary and ordinary individual with a frankly mediocre, even failed work history can look like a success. No one, it seems, can fail to benefit from the skill of their impression management professional. Read a peer's CV and the way he or she describes a modest achievement or mundane duty, and one can see the benefits of being economical with the truth.

Whilst this may be good for the job hunter, CVmanship certainly presents a problem for the selection and recruitment specialist. If all students are Einsteinian geniuses, all workers productive Stakanovites, all entrepreneurs neo-Bransons, how can one distinguish between them?

There are three important clues in the modern CV. First what is *left out*. Beware the CV which ignores or fudges chronicity: people may prefer to ignore long periods on the dole, a failed early career, an unwelcome start at one level. All sorts of important information may be omitted in the interests of the applicant. Selectors should perhaps have a checklist of information they really need and obtain it from the applicant if the CV does not provide it.

Second, there are the grand *generalisations*. 'My department had a $2 million budget' does not mean 'I was in charge of it'; 'Coordinated and facilitated staffing issues' could mean anything.

Third, there is the *verifiability* of the information. The more difficult it appears to check, the more likely it is a fudge. Beware the colo-

nial experience where applicants held impressive-sounding jobs, even
if they were genuine, in some far-flung outpost where their skin colour
and ability to speak English ensured them senior positions. A name
and address of organisations on the CV certainly helps a great deal.

The paradox of CVmanship is that there may well be an inverse
relationship between the CV and the person behind it. Over-egging
the pudding (bound glossy brochures with career histories spanning
several pages) screams the cumulative attempts of desperate outplacement consultants. The greater the flourish; the more the prizes; the
quicker the promotion – the more ordinary the individual.

26. Ability and Motivation are All You Need to be a High Flyer

Aspirants and selectors alike are fascinated by what it takes to
become a high flyer. Many different theories abound, some of which
are propounded in those curious autohagiographies of top tycoons.

Theories about *what it takes* stress all sorts of things: family background, particularly parental relationships and significant childhood
events; education at particular schools and universities; career
patterns emphasising the role of mentors etc.; task orientation
including work pattern and ethic; and finally that vaguest of all categories, philosophy of life.

Books with such titles as *Predicting Executive Success, The Change
Makers, Masters of Business* etc. tend to be long on speculation and
pomposity but short on insight.

Becoming a high flyer in management essentially takes three
things – ability, motivation and reputation. *All three* are required, in
varying amounts, depending on the particular field.

Clearly one needs ability to get on, though the precise nature of
this ability may differ from job to job, sector to sector, and time to
time. For some it is an ability with numbers, whereas for others it is
an ability with words. Some high flyers need to be able to think logically, other laterally. However, it isn't much use being an *idiot savant*,
i.e. being brilliant at one thing and practically nothing else. Despite
what some evangelical consultants might tell you about bolstering
self-esteem, believing in yourself and other 'air-head' hype, in order
to advance one does need to be able. This means certainly above
average on a range of salient attributes.

Next, that dustbin category for the hard-of-thinking in management circles – motivation. High flyers need to want to succeed; to be
motivated by the prize of the job whatever it may be (money, pres-

tige, power etc). Given the jungle of the marketplace, the sharp knives of organisational politics and the boxing ring of the executive committee, the high flyer needs to be driven. Some are *pushed* from memories of poverty, weakness or powerlessness, others are *pulled* by the high-flyer lifestyle of those they admire or emulate. The path is rocky and the journey long, hence endurance and fortitude are required. Never underestimate the power of motivation as a factor in success.

The third factor, unlike ability, can be acquired, but is a delicate plant not totally under one's control. It is reputation. Shrewd people realise the importance of cultivating, maintaining and occasionally boosting a good reputation. A reputation for fairness, hard work and competence is always desirable, but often a reputation for certain less desirable qualities does no harm and may in fact be beneficial. To be tough, aggressive, intolerant of fools and unsympathetic may at times be a case of praising with faint damns. Some marketing-oriented and shrewd people put a great deal of effort into nurturing a certain image and reputation, be it true or not. And that, of course, is the odd point about reputation – its correlation with actuality may be very slight indeed.

Clearly each of the above three factors is not enough on its own. Nor is it good enough merely to have two out of three. To be able and motivated, but without any reputation, may mean that you are not noticed. To be able and with a good and helpful reputation, but without much motivation, means you may be too reluctant to make the move that leads to success. And to be motivated and of good repute yet without ability surely means you are the victim of the Peter Principle.

One can go a long way with two-thirds of what one really needs to make it. And, of course, we haven't listed that old favourite mentioned most frequently by the less successful – luck. Yes, success is an ABC: ability, breaks and courage. But, as Vidal Sassoon noted, 'The only place where success comes before work is in the dictionary'.

27. There are Big Sex Differences at Work

Suggesting that there are sex differences in anything these days is sensitive stuff. It is bad enough to suggest that they exist, let alone to argue that they are a result of biological differences (and hence unchangeable) rather than learnt (and hence un- or re-learnable).

Do men and women have different expectations and experiences at work? We are, as it happens, short on neither myths nor data about the issue. Myths abound on this topic, e.g. that when dissatisfied at work, men go on strike and women go absent. Or that the physical and social environment at work is more important to women compared with men, whilst men more than women are concerned with job pay and job titles.

The only way to separate fact from fiction and myth from reality is by consulting the data. In order to see whether women and men see and experience work differently one needs answers to a comprehensive, valid and sensitive set of questions from a large, representative population. Researchers in this area have confirmed all sorts of ideas, e.g:

- Females rate pleasant colleagues/peers and working conditions as more important than do males. Males rate job variety, challenge, responsibility and participation as more important than do females.
- Females tend to be more satisfied than males with respect to pay because females have lower expectations.
- Females prefer people-oriented, caring sorts of jobs more than males.

The problem with all surveys in this area is that many do not take into consideration other confounding factors that may be different between male and female employees and which are the real cause of the difference noted. Females populate organisations but rarely run them. Ambitious, competent and hard-working female managers talk of the 'glass ceiling': a covert barrier to advancement. There are powerful forces that continue to operate against females in work settings. These include:

- *Sex Role Stereotypes*: It is still a widespread belief that males tend to be aggressive, forceful, persistent and decisive whereas females are passive, intuitive, dependent and emotional. Self-fulfilling prophets in selection, recruitment and promotion usually find it easy enough to confirm their beliefs and keep women in the canteen, the personnel department or behind the PA's PC!
- *Expectations*: It does seem that females hold lower expectations (for instance about starting pay and peak salary) than males, possibly because they specialise in lower paid jobs or indeed observe the world around them. It is a truism but true that people tend to get what they expect and thus females themselves fulfil their own prophecies.

• *Self-confidence.* 'Bullshit baffles brains' might be graffiti but in business self-confidence is one of the best predictors of organisational success. Although it may be changing, females frequently express lower self-confidence than males in many achievement situations, and therefore don't achieve.

Thus it is that in most organisations males, compared with females, occupy higher positions, are better paid, have better promotion opportunities, have more power, control and responsibility and consequently get more perks.

If you compare the beliefs and behaviours of males and females in an organisation you are likely to find quite a few differences. The *National Organisation Audit* performed by Barrie Gunter and me looked at the corporate culture and climate of different organisations. We did find in various organisations that females reported less job variety, less influence, less involvement in decision making, less training, and less of a feeling that they knew what was going on. Yet there was still comparatively little difference between the sexes, compared with differences between age-groups or different grade levels. In fact once we controlled for grade, education, salary etc. those few sex differences almost completely disappeared.

Optimists would probably prefer to concentrate on those areas where no or minimal differences were apparent whereas pessimists (or realists?) might choose to highlight the major differences between the two sexes. It is of course quite possible that numerous subtle but important differences do exist between the sexes in what they want from work, but it is equally clear that the similarities far outweigh the differences.

It is one thing to know that these differences (and similarities) exist but quite another to explain them. It is probably true, as Golda Meir remarked, 'To be successful, a woman has to be better at her job than a man' but then, for the world of work, 'a woman who strives to be a man lacks ambition'. There are a few sex differences in the workplace which we perhaps should celebrate rather than lament. However, we now have the data to test some of the more horny chauvinist and feminist theories. Predictably perhaps, both appear too simplistic.

28. You Can't Predict or Explain the Personality Clash

There are two types of people in the world: those who believe there are two types and those who don't. Those who do have developed all sorts of categories and labels: introverts and extroverts, thinkers and doers, boffins and generalists, barrow-boys and toffs.

Supposedly, the 'opposite' types don't like, understand or respect each other. People talk about a personality clash. But what does this mean and why does it occur?

The term 'personality clash' appears to mean that two people don't share the same values, preferences and attitudes or, more mundanely, how they go about their work. Larks or morning types loathe four o'clock meetings and believe owls do not work after 5:30, whilst the latter are never sure, and can't confirm, precisely when the larks arrive at the office or what, if anything, they do then.

The concept of personality clash does not come from the psychologist's and psychiatrist's lexicon. But psychologists, consultants and trainers, eager for eponymous fame (and a quick buck) have made endless distinctions and devised innumerable tests to measure the two types. Note that nearly always two opposing types are defined; ideal for the clash.

Psychobabble terms abound in this ego-satisfying world of self-discovery, where on training courses participants are encouraged to assess and appraise their own style. Sometimes, though by no means always, their opposite type is also described or explained, presumably to help or diffuse a personality clash.

Many of the distinctions made revolve around a very limited number of simple but important differences. The first is as much discussed as it is not understood. It involves seeking arousal, stimulation and variety.

Consider the malfunctioning motor car: some cut out at the lights, requiring more petrol and a richer mix; others over-rev. The one needs more, the other less fuel. Extroverts – those outgoing, sociable, impulsive types – are physically underaroused and seek continual stimulation. Because people have one thing in common, that is they are all different, they are a good source of stimulation. Extroverts trade off accuracy for speed in their search for excitement. No wonder, then, that they are more likely to have accidents, more likely to break the law, more likely to take drugs and smoke. The exhibitionist thrill-seeking of the extroverts is as biologically hard-wired as the peace-seeking of the introverts, quite content with a book, a chess game or a stroll in the fields. Physiologically over-aroused, the introvert is as stressed by more stimulation as the extrovert is pleased.

Hence the extrovert sees the introvert as boring, inadequate and secretive, whilst the latter sees the former as attention seeking, shallow and noisy. The two extremes choose different environments to do differently-preferred jobs with colleagues of their own type. Ambiverts, to use the correct term for those of us in the middle of the spectrum, tend to get on fairly well with both types as long as they are not too extreme.

Another important distinction concerns essentially whether one is task or people oriented. Task-oriented people tend to be procedures and systems driven, rule oriented and attracted to technology. They focus on the here-and-now practicalities of the task, they like logical analysis, and they see themselves as sensible. Dedicated, sometimes autocratic, they make excellent scientists, engineers and accountants. And they tend to clash with those managers who focus not on the task but on people and relationships. Relationship people might prefer a zealous missionary management style and are focused on the future. Many prefer the possible to the practical; the 'what if' to the 'what is'; intuition to facts. They are the creatives of marketing and advertising agencies; the people managers of big corporations.

The tough, no-funny-business, task-oriented manager sees his/her opposite as impractical, even incompetent, a hopeless dreamer rather than a solid worker. The intuitive, people-oriented manager, on the other hand, sees his/her opposite as a mechanical dullard enslaved to the bureaucratic tedium of the current system. The two types despise each other and hate to work under any regime imposed by the preferences of their opposites.

'Personality clash' is not just a polite, non-technical term for mutual dislike or distrust, or even about having different value systems and prejudices. Personality clashes occur because people have strong inbuilt preferences for how they should behave at work. And they tend to take great exception to those who express opposite preferences *and* have the power to enforce them.

29. Big is Beautiful in Business

Management scientists and business gurus, or others interested in organisational or corporate behaviour, observe and study companies in much the same way as anthropologists study exotic and primitive tribes. They attempt to understand the nature, function and symbolic meaning of dress, rituals and meetings, showing how the everyday is imbued with meaning.

There used to be a time when there was a positive association between one's power and status in an organisation and the size of one's desk. All cartoons still show dictatorial, merchant-baron captains of industry seated behind half an acre of polished oak, glaring at a clearly intimidated employee. The desk is relatively bare except for a few expensive executive toys and trinkets.

The imagery is clear: size was equated with power. But, more importantly, in all desks there were drawers, trays, files and various other 'clever little niches' to store papers and other documents. The grand old roll-top desk with a veritable bank of storage compartments was the best example of this genre. Information was power. It was stored on paper in cardboard files. The more of these documents and files one had, the more powerful one was. But now desks are out and tables are in.

Further, the shape and size of the 'designer' table reflects a rather different image. Frequently they are oval or occasionally circular, rarely oblong, never square. Often their surface is bare, though the room should contain a computer terminal, one telephone, a couple of good pieces of art (never a portrait or certificates of degrees), a few comfortable chairs and a couch. Colours should preferably be pale so as to heighten the effect of openness. The crucial image, it seems, is one of space, lack of clutter, indeed a minimalist emptiness.

The briefcase – a sort of mobile desk – is an ideal corporate cultural icon worthy of study. It certainly comes in many forms. First, there is the shabby, donnish, somewhat battered leather bag. Shapeless and scarred, it is usually large so that it can contain simultaneously books, papers, overnight clothes and perhaps even the odd sandwich. Its shapelessness is primarily due to its being stretched by odd contents (e.g. tennis rackets, a computer, books and papers). Then there are those fairly large square cases – the more hideous made of plastic (or some substitute) – designed not to be flexible but to have useful compartments for felt-tipped pens. Third, there is the 'expensive material' designer case that follows no shape rule except that it is made out of crocodile, calf or some other unfortunate animal. Each of these cases may have monograms or initials and a lock, both of which are, or rather were, a modest sign of status.

Now, however, status is distinguished not so much by shape or material, but size. Capable of carrying only the *Financial Times*, the new wafer-thin briefcase is remarkable for not looking like a briefcase at all. The less one can carry in the case, the better.

But why have the larger desk and the solid briefcase been replaced by the designer table and a briefcase as thin as a folder? The answer lies in the way in which we now use, store and gain access to information. The higher one rises within an organisation, the more one becomes a pure administrator. Generals don't fight, professors don't teach, bishops don't convert...they all administer in the sense that they are decision makers. These experts have been briefed by the underlings. Each in turn has had to condense information about sales, grants, movements etc. from vast printouts into pretty (preferably coloured) computer graphics of pie charts, histograms etc. – a sort of visual image for the hard-of-thinking. The higher one is in the organisation, the more this interpretation and selection of data are required and the more they are boiled down.

Around the conference table, then, the decision maker may call for information about a particular issue. This information has no doubt been carried to the meeting by the lieutenant, in a briefcase slightly bigger than that of the person above him. And this briefing has already occurred at various levels, each time with an underling providing more and more material and printouts which the person above selects, edits and summarises and so reduces in size. Thus, as with the porters of David Livingstone and Edmund Hillary, the more one carries, the lowlier one is. To misquote the Duchess of Windsor: 'one can never be too rich or one's briefcase too thin'.

30. It's Easy Adapting to Working Abroad

One of the many consequences of Empire is that the emigrant British diaspora is amazingly widespread. Some countries such as America, Australia and South Africa may have together millions of British passport holders of which a good percentage think of themselves as expats.

From Kota Kinabalo to Karachi, and from Bridgetown to Bloemfontein, one can 'unearth' the British expat. Some may be in the chameleon disguise of the native whilst others are conspicuously and proudly British, going out in the midday sun. Others talk consistently of home and live according to seasonal patterns quite out of synchrony with the local time.

The expats can be found at the country club famous for its poor food, cheap gin and faithful retainers. But they can also be found in the local church, the Rotary Club, the WI and the British Council. Others are not so obvious, preferring either to blend in with the locals or keep very much to themselves.

But how do the British adapt to living and working abroad? Are they uniquely effective expats or is it true that, like American jokes and Bulgarian wine, they don't travel well?

An expat is usually definable as someone who makes the decision to live and work abroad. He/she should have some choice in the matter and be of an age to be self-sufficient. Many an expat starts out as an *adventurer* – someone who, at a relatively young age, with few responsibilities and a taste for sensation seeking, set out abroad 'for a while'. Many don't plan to be expats but find themselves in the role. But how do they change over time? What happens to these fleeing bounty seekers?

It seems various ways of adapting are open to them. These different styles may change over time and indeed they may be more common in some countries than others. But most are immediately recognisable.

1. *Upwardly Mobile.* This expat soon discovers that with some technical training, a western education, English fluency and a white skin they are top of the pecking order. In demographic speak a C2, *Daily Mirror* reader is treated like an A or B socio-economic group member. Instead of being a servant, one has servants; instead of taking orders one gives them. And it's a good feeling; so much so that return becomes unthinkable because it means downward mobility.

2. *Sojourners.* This group is more pragmatic, with a long-term plan. They are abroad for a specific goal and usually a set time period. It may be to accrue capital to pay off a mortgage or start a small business. Or it may be to do one's duty in the company and earn promotion on return. These are, strictly speaking, not expats but temporary sojourners on a foreign posting, though they usually mix with expats.

3. *Nomads.* These are sequential sojourners in the sense that they pitch their tent in one country after another apparently aimlessly. A new pasture seems to be all they are after for they follow no long-term plan. The relative buoyancy of national economics may be enough to spur a move as they trade the bear market for that of the bull. But the longer they spend abroad the harder it is to go home. They are condemned to being the wandering albatrosses of the expat world.

4. *Financially Trapped.* This group is one of the saddest. They have stayed too long at a place in decline. They do not have the option to return 'home' because they are tied into a pension plan and indeed a weak economy. The financially trapped may be found in badly managed, newly independent countries where the currency has been chronically devalued. They cannot move or come home because they simply have no capital. Whilst they may be 'all right' if they stay put, their lack of

foresight or simple bad luck has meant they are condemned to exile.

5. *Gone Troppo*. One of the most curious and perhaps pathetic reactions of the long-term expat is when he or she has gone native. This may be quaint or downright peculiar. It is, of course, much more than becoming thoroughly acquainted with the language, the dress codes and the norms of the natives but is a rejection of one's own values. This is not the stuff of the White Rajas but more that of Lawrence of Arabia. More often, however, it can look pathetic and may be induced as much by a love of alcohol and adultery as by the values and behavioural norms of the local culture.

6. *The Never Lefts*. The most odd reaction is that of the expats who behave as if they never left Sevenoaks or Sunningdale. They may be marooned in a tropical paradise, or isolated in the primitive bush but they are slavishly faithful to their old ways of dress, food, social behaviour. Caught in time, they maintain the style and preferences of the country they left which now no longer exist. The past is indeed another country.

Colonialism may have been replaced by 'Coca-Colanialism' but in some places the expats exist as if nothing has changed since the great days of empire. They are happy to be abroad so long as the natives are waiters and drivers. And many have a deeply ambivalent attitude to the mother country and the thought of coming home. To re-pat the expat is indeed a major challenge.

Chapter 6: Myths about Control

- Administration: The art of looking for trouble, finding it whether it exists or not, diagnosing it incorrectly and applying the wrong remedy.
- Running a business these days is like Dudley Moore dancing with Racquel Welch. The overhead is fantastic.
- Most success comes from ignoring the obvious (Trevor Holdsworth).
- We are tough and brave in war. We are soft and compromising in management (Sir Michael Edwardes).
- Dreams have their place in managerial ability, but they need to be kept severely under control (Lord Weinstock).
- I can't stand this proliferation of paperwork. It's useless to fight the forms. You've got to kill the people producing them (Vladamir Kabaidze).

Managers have to understand, appraise and discipline their staff. Some attempt to do it themselves; others pass it on to those in the HR function. Some managers are more interested than others in measuring performance and giving feedback to their staff in the hope that they will improve.

But are managers the only people in a position to give feedback? Who knows the manager's style, strengths, foibles and failures best: his/her boss or staff? The answer is nearly always the staff. Are they therefore not in a good position to rate their boss and give him/her honest, accurate and useful feedback? Managers can also be rated by their clients/customers, shareholders and colleagues. Their different, aggregated feedback enriches the total picture of management behaviour.

There remains considerable controversy over whether punishment, sometimes called discipline, works. There are those who argue that just as all animal trainers only use reward to train their beasts to do amazing (if pointless) tasks, so man-managers should do likewise. But there are those too who believe in firm discipline. And there are managers who, though they don't like it, are forced in their own eyes to use discipline when all other methods fail.

Another response of some managers is to send their 'real' problem cases to the personnel or human resources department, which is seen as the specialist in employee problems. But there are those who believe the precise opposite – that so-called personnel specialists are not a help but an expensive hindrance. They are a costly, pointless overhead. What role does the middle manager play in the organisation? Some believe they serve precious little function, except to create work for themselves, and that they merit culling. Others believe their experience and knowledge are invaluable to the organisation. The middle-aged middle manager, however, is an endangered species: rightsizing and restructuring mean they are very vulnerable to the axe.

Managing a big workforce usually means dealing with people whose age range varies from school leavers to post-retirees. Do age-gaps make a difference? They do in families but surely not in the world of work. But as different generations have been brought up with very different attitudes to work so these shine through in the workplace and have to be managed.

31. Managers are the Best Appraisers of Employee Performance

Managing performance involves, by definition, evaluation and rating. In competitive leisure activities, as in the world of work, judgements of worth, excellence or ability have to be made. Whether the activity is growing and showing roses, disciplining and exhibiting dogs, or blending and tasting wines, a judgement of quality and quantity is required. The question is, who is best suited to make the most astute but impartial judgement?

Few jobs or competitive hobbies have a clear, first-past-the-post way of assessing success. The Darwinian rules of survival of the fittest may work, but only over the long term. And because people need feedback on their performance, they have to be evaluated along a continuum of dimensions.

From a very early age we are given tests of our ability, knowledge and skill which are rated by parents, teachers and peers. School exams, driving tests and assessment centres all involve the rating of performance.

Performance can be rated in many ways. Sometimes it can be done by machines which can measure strength, fitness etc. Machines can also accurately score multiple-choice answers on a test by laser reading of the pencil marks. But, as we all know, the more subtle, important, and higher-level skills, abilities and products cannot be rated by multiple-choice objective tests. No chemistry analysis can discriminate a great wine; no simple selection test can infallibly choose the best CEO.

But given that someone has to make a judgement, the question remains: *who* should that be? An expert, one's superiors, one's colleagues, one's friends (reference writers)?

Who should be the judge of one's work performance? Tradition- ally it is a superior – usually the person to whom you report, possibly the boss. But it could equally be a peer. Even more radically it could be a subordinate or, for greater reliability, a whole group of them. Why not be evaluated by your customers – and don't say you don't have any! What about your shareholders? The idea of customers or share- holders judging senior managers sends a shudder down the spines of most people but it could be argued that these groups *are* making judge- ments of our performance all the time, even if not explicitly.

Different groups of raters have quite different perspectives and therefore sources of bias. In the jargon of experimental science one needs multitrait, multirater appraisal. That means evaluation of various traits (or behaviours, or skills) by various people to be most accurate. Consider the advantages to the average middle manager of being rated by his/her boss, peers, subordinates, customers, share- holders (if appropriate) and possibly a self-rating on various work- related behaviours.

For most, self-evaluation is out because it leads to self-aggrandise- ment and delusional high scores. Some people give themselves unfair and unrealistic positive halos, whereas the depressed and morbidly self-critical do the very opposite and give themselves extremely low scores. Both are inaccurate and poor discriminators.

Most employees are rated by their bosses. He/she supposedly knows their virtues and faults, strengths and weaknesses, abilities and foibles. That may well be true if one has a sensitive, perceptive boss with not too large a span of control. For many people, the quality and quantity of interaction with their boss is so low that there is really no possibility of sensitive and accurate judgements being made.

What about your peers? Some studies have found they are amongst the most accurate and predictive of judges. Research on officers' training corps and other high-powered assessment centres found, when asked, that the participants were better predictors of success than the judges themselves. Why? Simply because the peers had more opportunity to observe all the antics of their colleagues during the 'up-front', more public times and also during the 'backstage' activities.

Some organisations are risking upward feedback – that is, feedback from subordinates. This may be inaccurate either because subordinates have an axe to grind (leading to very negative evaluations) or are sycophantic and boot-licking (leading to positive evaluation). None the less it is subordinates who experience and therefore know the consequences of a manager's behaviour. And if all subordinates give similar ratings, this is surely a testament to reliability.

Service jobs have external customers and it is not uncommon for them to be asked to rate performance. Hotels, banks, airlines and restaurants are used to doing this. How seriously those ratings are taken varies in practice but the principle is a good one.

Much is now made of 360-degree feedback or ratings from top, bottom and both sides. In theory this must be a good idea as long as the raters are trained and the rating dimensions are relevant to the job. All examiners need to be trained and their criteria need to be salient to the skill or performance evaluated. Given these conditions (often not fully considered), multiple raters help to remove the bias and subjectivity in the whole process.

32. Discipline is Never the Last Resort

How do you get more out of your employees? How can the average manager acquire a hard-working, loyal, motivated, enthusiastic and adaptable workforce? What do you have to do as manager to achieve maximum results from your staff?

The bookshelves of many managers are a testament to increasing disillusionment as one series of fix-it books is replaced by another. Rather than seeing increasing sophistication over time as old ideas and methods are discarded, improved upon or fine-tuned, one witnesses one fashionable idea simply being replaced by another. However, usually there is a discernible trend which starts with emphasis on the importance of selection and ends with the belief that only discipline will really work. For some, at one end of this spectrum, it is purely a matter of selecting the best people in the first place. This group of managers believes that there are fundamental, significant and longstanding differences between individuals which powerfully affect their behaviour at work. Thus they place great faith, and are prepared to invest consequent amounts of money, in assessment centres, psychometric testing, or in-house interviewing. Those who believe in selection as a royal road to success believe it is quite possible accurately to choose the good and reject the bad, and that 'good' candidates will become 'good' employees for the rest of their careers.

The next school is less enthralled by selection, because it is believed to be too costly, too difficult or even not that important. They believe, along with the Catholics, that given a person at an appropriate stage in their organisational socialisation, they can be trained to be the sort of employee who is sought after. The training-oriented are thus prepared to invest large amounts of money in training units, training consultants or business-school programmes.

The more military-minded types are more concerned with organisational *structure*, reporting lines and clear rules for behaviour. They insist that employees knowing what their jobs are, where they fit into the organisation, who they receive orders from and who they give orders to are the crucial features to ensure employee success. Hence they are happy to have their organisation restructured, job descriptions rewritten and rules redrafted every so often in order to guarantee that their own particular 'secret of success' is put in place.

The latest magic charm for some is 'corporate culture'. Although uncertain about the real meaning or manifestation of this term, some managers are certain this is the key to success. Hence they commission expensive corporate culture audits, ponder over the results, decide their 'wannabees' and set about culture change programmes. This may involve strange simulated exercises in unfamiliar hotels or dramatic rule changes in the organisation, all aimed to induce a radically changed behaviour set in the hapless employee.

In fact for many managers, and especially the world-weary and battered middle-aged, middle-brow middle managers, there is a history of personal disillusionment as they were convinced of, invested in and tried out various solutions (selection, training, etc.), only to find them ultimately unsuccessful, or not the panacea they were promised. The optimists turn into pessimists, the believers in the essential goodness and honesty of people into those convinced that nearly all workers are lazy, feckless and stupid.

So they resort to the final solution – the stick of *discipline* which may come in many forms. Having possibly tried each of the above approaches in turn and been convinced that they do not work, the exasperated and depressed manager often turns to the old standby of the disciplinary interview, the final warning and all the symbolism of punishment. The fact that discipline does not work either seems to matter little. Often it is simply retributive, like prison.

The problem, of course, is that no one solution works perfectly. There is no quick-fix, magic bullet, simple HR success formula, despite all the business magazine hype. All methods – the old as well as the new – work to some extent. And, perhaps more importantly, they can be applied simultaneously rather than sequentially.

The weary, embittered manager who is too fond of disciplinary threats may once have been a naive optimist searching for *the* answer to all managerial problems. And that search is ultimately like that for the Holy Grail: long, complicated, infused with myth and doomed to failure.

33. Nearly all Organisations Value the HR Function

The term 'Human Resources' is pronounced 'Overhead'. Human resources staff, it is often said, are costly, bureaucratic, unresponsive time-wasters who don't add value. Worse, HR people who don't understand the business try to interfere with operations.

Some people maintain that HR stands for Human Remains: the left-over sideways-moved people. In his humorous and controversial book *Up the Organisation*, Townsend says the first thing one should do is fire the whole HR department. He says the same of the PR department and is clearly intending to shock. But many share his sentiments, particularly when take-over, restructuring and downsizing occur.

Fast trackers avoid a stint in HR. To many line managers, 'personnel Johnnies' appear to be a bunch of drones whose apparent missions in life are to create paperwork, recruit secretaries who can't type and issue memos whose impertinence is only exceeded by their irrelevance. As a result, personnel directors, whatever their individual competence, suffer the image of being harmless 'old farts' who spend their careers worshipping files, devising pointless programmes and generally accomplishing nothing of any fundamental importance.

All HR is essentially management of people. But all managers are involved in managing people and the management of an organisation's staff is primarily a line or operating management responsibility.

The degree, however, to which HR activities are divided between line or operating managers and the HR manager and his or her department varies from organisation to organisation.

In some organisations, a human resource specialist may handle all negotiations with unions, whereas in others operating managers may see union negotiations as their responsibility with the HR manager taking an advisory role, or having no involvement at all. Line managers in some organisations are now starting to compete with HR specialists to assume responsibility for many traditional HR activities.

In this sense HR people become redundant because their jobs are now taken over by newly empowered and better educated managers who are taught HR processes and procedures before or while in the job. According to some writers, if the HR specialists are to survive and indeed thrive, they need to obey certain crucial rules:

1. The HR function should always be carried out as close to the operational sharp end as is feasible.
2. The HR 'strategy and policy' function should always be carried out as close to the strategy and policy decision maker as possible.
3. The HR function should never have 'line' authority – its only power should be through influence via its know-how, skills and expertise.
4. An HR professional who craves real direct authority should become a line manager and not compromise the HR function's real task.
5. The best manager of human resources is rarely the head of the HR department.
6. The best manager of human resources is a line manager who is a natural or is well trained.

HR professionals must, like all others (marketing, manufacturing, finance), understand the importance of, be sensitive to, and actually help in achieving bottom-line targets. This may therefore involve downsizing, instituting Pay for Performance schemes and attempting to demonstrate the cost efficiency of training. All HR departments are of course also responsible for:

*   *Cost containment*: HR objectives and activities should *genuinely* focus on cost reduction via reduced head count and improved expense control. Indeed HR departments should themselves model the 'lean and mean' department.

- *Customer service:* HR activities should aim to achieve improved customer service through recruitment and selection, employee training and development, rewards and motivation etc. Again, the department should have an eye on its own internal and external customers and seek out their feedback regularly.
- *Social responsibility:* HR objectives should centre on legal compliance and achieving improvements in areas such as equal opportunity, occupational health and safety and development programmes, whilst bearing in mind that their organisation is neither a charity nor uncritical of political correctness.
- *Organisational effectiveness:* HR should focus on organisational structure, employee motivation, employee innovation, adaptability to change, flexible reward systems, employee relations and so on.

The old-style personnel manager (often a retired military officer) has evolved into a sophisticated human resource professional. Managed properly, the HR function should demonstrate to the rest of the organisation that, rather than being a waste of space, it is a significant contributor to company strategy.

34. Most Middle Managers are Pretty Redundant

It is difficult to imagine any British manager except the media-illiterate or resolutely ostrich-like who is ignorant of some of the major buzzwords of the HR whizz-kids.

In the fashion-conscious and ephemeral world of management consultancies and human resource departments, various 'new' ideas and concepts promise to be the magic bullet for all management problems. The business gurus and consultants argue that 'if you only do XYZ, all your problems will be over'.

The gullible, the stressed and the plainly desperate middle-aged, middle-brow and middle-ranking manager is often relieved and delighted to receive this news. And so he/she attends seminars, has consultants set up workshops and action teams and goes about making the changes in the hope that they will cure all ills.

Three ideas, concepts or models – call them what you will depending on your need for embellishment – are currently floating about. One is *empowerment*, an ugly transatlantic neologism, which suggests that ordinary workers want, enjoy and benefit from empowerment. Of course, with power comes responsibility, and it is not clear that workers who warm to the former are equally happy about the latter. Also, the empowerment of one group usually means the disempowerment of another group, frequently the former's bosses. And there's the rub.

The next idea is *delayering*, which is a simple but enormously consequential structural issue. For all sorts of reasons, including obvious ones such as a set span of control, many organisations are very tall with many ranks, levels or layers. Armies are always a quintessential example. Now we are told this is inefficient, wasteful and redundant. Examples are held up such as the Catholic Church which, despite its size, has only three or four levels under its CEO, the Bishop of Rome. So the preferred solution, and one which can be achieved with a stroke of the pen on the organisational chart, is to take out one, two or more levels of management.

The next idea, borrowed from the tough, masculine, no-nonsense world of heavy industry is *re-engineering*. Though, as in all of these concepts, there is some disagreement as to the precise meaning of the term, it implies that organisations need to be structurally and functionally redesigned. Just as the old, complicated steam engine was re-engineered into the sleek bullet train, so elaborate, traditional organisations can be streamlined. And this usually means removal of many jobs consequently perceived as redundant.

What these three new ideas have in common is that they usually lead to a similar result, which, because of its unpleasantness, has a number of euphemisms including 'downsizing', 'retrenchment' and 'redeployment'. In the words of the blunt, these new-fangled ideas usually mean the sacking of middle management.

Is this culling a good idea? Are most middle managers Peter-principled, disengaged and therefore really pretty redundant? If so, why did that position arise in the first place? What is the role of someone between the front-line supervisor and the directors?

In some organisations, middle managers will not be missed because senior or top managers were performing their jobs. The owners directed, the directors managed, the managers supervised, the supervisors worked. The job of directors and top managers is predominantly planning, i.e. forward looking and 'visionary'. The job of the supervisor is primarily operational, day-to-day management.

About 70% of the time of the former is about thinking ahead and doing work that cannot be delegated, whilst about the same amount of the time of the latter is working with and through people at the coal-face.

The middle manager, the departmental head, the divisional chief and the coordinator supposedly did some planning, some man-management and even practised some of the skills for which they had been trained. Some, of course, were simply bureaucrats, some against any change which threatened their stability, and some simply incompetent.

Perhaps most organisations simply had too many middle managers and a bit of judicious pruning was rather a good idea. But to remove a whole level, or layer, or generation, may be exceptionally foolhardy, at least until its function is fully understood.

35. There are no Generation Gaps at Work

Most big organisations have a highly heterogeneous workforce. People of different ages, backgrounds and education levels perform a variety of tasks in teams, sections and departments.

It is often the case that the better educated are at the top of the organisation, doing the more conceptual work. Some would argue that various glass, or even steel, ceilings actually prevent people with certain characteristics, based on gender, skin colour or religious persuasion, from rising up the corporate ladder.

Oxbridge WASPS, a highly homogeneous group, still run the show even in Mr Major's egalitarian Britain, but lower down the ladder there is more variety. It is therefore not uncommon to find people from different age-groups doing much the same job, particularly at lower levels in middle management.

What is it like to manage people from different age-groups? What effect has their early upbringing had on their approach to work? Are older people more conscientious and younger people more hypochondriacal, or the other way around? Has the work ethic died among the postwar baby-boomers? Do the young have ambitions they can't achieve and the old reminiscences of things that never happened?

Everyone brings to their workplace expectations shaped by experience in the wider society. The great depression; the war; the rebellious swinging sixties; the oil-crisis-induced recession of the seventies; the ebullient triumphalist years of Thatcher; these experiences live with people. They come to expect, demand and thus create a work environment that fulfils those expectations.

It seems that for people aged between 20 and 60 there are five different cohorts, each shaped by their shared experiences.

- The depression of the 1930s made a strong impression on people. They grew up in the world of hard knocks and they valued above everything else a steady job to insure against the vicissitudes of misfortune. This generation accepted that work involved fairly boring specified routines, strict discipline and a recognition that promotion is based on seniority.

- The war years required that people make sacrifices for a better life. People became used to working in teams and some, such as the newly working women, saw their work as a challenge. Many liked the freedom to operate and experiment with new ways of doing things. They remember the adventure and now, providing they have 'comrades', are prepared to try something new.

- Children of the 1950s benefited from social stability and economic growth. They tend to see work as an opportunity to engage in meaningful acts and stress getting along well with co-workers. Many are concerned with equity and fairness in the workplace but may be rather conservative in their views.

- The swinging sixties children had the economic benefits of growth and wealth. Not only did they challenge authority and accepted truths, but they also experienced threats posed by pollution, racial disturbances and nuclear war. This generation did not believe in organisational commitment. Living for the day, they looked for rapid promotion and immediate recognition. Many of these young people believed that work can and should be satisfying, fun and rewarding and seemed surprised when their near-impossible expectations were not fulfilled. However, the oil crisis in the 1970s and the grim industrial debates made some turn sour.

- Thatcher's children are a lot more sober about work. Knowing the hardship of unemployment, they yearn for stability and security more than excitement. But they are also advocates of the principle of equity over equality and favour performance-related pay.

Dramatic technological innovations and increasing wealth have meant that people are better paid for working fewer hours under immeasurably better conditions. Most generations believe their successors to be lazier, greedier, less disciplined, possibly better educated but undeservingly more ambitious than themselves. As Oscar Wilde observed, 'The old believe everything; the middle-aged suspect everything; the young know everything'.

Of course, most managers want a young person's flexibility, desire and ability to learn, a middle-aged person's perseverance and tenacity and an older worker's commitment and stoicism. Some industries seem to believe in trading off some of these virtues, one against the other, by choosing the workforce from a specific age-group. Others have no choice when the skills, training and abilities they seek are found only in one generation and that is often the youngest.

Chapter 7:
Myths about
Experts

- Expert: An ordinary guy 50 miles from home.
- Changing a business requires dynamite and it's a consultant who lights the fuse (S. Sakanoto).
- Consultant: Someone who knows less about your business than you, but who gets more out of it by telling you what he knows than you do if you work the right way instead of doing what he tells you.
- I find it rather easy to portray a businessman. Being bland, rather cruel and incompetent comes naturally to me (John Cleese).
- I come from an environment where, if you see a snake, you kill it. At General Motors, if you see a snake, the first thing you do is hire a consultant on snakes (Ross Perot).

Business is full of all sorts of experts. Both from within the organisation but increasingly from without there is no shortage of people happy to use that expert knowledge, skill and invoices to help. But do people like or trust experts?

As public relations experts are quick to point out, the public are a wary lot. Better educated, assertive and very sensitive to being hoodwinked, the ordinary citizen is deeply sceptical, nay cynical about the motives, honesty and even the expertise of the experts.

Consultants might be feared, loathed and despised by many but they continue to flourish. They are often both perpetuators and victims of fashions, trends and jargon. They are, or at least sound, convinced that some new technique – often quite simple but rarely cheap or easy to supply – is the single solution to all problems and woes. But what would happen if one did the precise opposite of what they recommended?

Experts seek money, power and fame. One of the greatest accolades is to have a law or principle named after us. Curiously nearly all the famous ones in management describe not the principles of success but those of failure. It would seem that fame results from pointing out human foibles and fallacies rather than strengths.

Many experts base their diagnoses on surveys or interviews. They are a cheap way of gathering useful data. Managing directors, like politicians, might pretend not to pay attention to polls but most secretly rely heavily on them in their decision making. But are they accurate?

One way to see the power of experts is to see how they can market what is a dreary uncomfortable experience and present it as a romantic dream. Being confined in a small seat, in dry, recycled air in a wide steel pipe for 10–12 hours could be seen as a perverse form of torture. But the experts have portrayed air travel as an exotic, desirable experience. How have they done that? Read on.

36. Most Employees Trust Experts

For most of us, all the authority figures in whom we use to trust and believe have lost much of their credibility. The local GP and the parish priest are no longer the voices of authority. Politicians and law enforcers have suffered a dent to their pride and credibility.

Academics are no longer seen as objective, detached and well informed as they use to be. Business consultants have long, and in many people's eyes deservedly, been ridiculed and have to win their expertise spurs with each new client.

But one group, some of whom are rather naive in the spotlight, has seen its credibility (and hence self-respect) drop spectacularly. These are the scientists. It is scientists vs the people on some television programmes, and, rather than listening in awed and respectful silence, Joe Public argues and even sometimes succeeds in humiliating the boffins. Neither trusted nor respected, scientists are frequently stereotyped as callous, calculating or simply interpersonally inadequate.

Equally, 'personalities' seem to carry more weight than professionals. Film and sports stars, despite their lack of education or information on highly technical topics, are seen as more honest than professionals who are 'trained to know'. So activist groups now command the high ground despite their sometimes obscure funding, implicit ideologies and dubious methods. A nuclear protester is believed more than a nuclear scientist; a consumer protectionist more than a company's occupational medical health officer.

Many in-house managers, and even PR managers, say 'The trouble is, the public don't understand us'. But the obverse is true: they do not understand the public and how to inform them.

Imagine that you are the CEO of a new chemical factory and your local community groups are beginning to express fear and hostility to your operation. Journalists are snooping about and there is even talk of a consumer boycott of your products. What should you do? Sack the company's PR spokesperson? Commission a scientific review? Circulate factual press releases? Call a community meeting? Deny everything via lawyers? Keep your head down and ignore the issue? Organise tours of your factory to show how safe it is? Attempt to bribe the protestors with various gifts to the local community?

One of the most common strategies is also the least effective. It could be described as the rational method, i.e. explaining the probability of risk. Try telling a flying phobic that flying is safer than crossing the road. It might be true but it doesn't help.

If people believe something to be dangerous it is difficult to persuade them otherwise. They tend too often to shoot the messenger who nearly always downplays the risk and danger by providing correct but fairly indigestible comparative data on risks of all sorts. But what these experts or company representatives do not say is what they are doing to reduce the risk, to prevent accidents and to cope with emergencies. The public are not asking for zero risks. Whilst they would prefer not to recognise that no activity is risk free, they are not naive.

By and large, when dealing with the public, four steps are necessary. First, it is essential to acknowledge that some risk does exist. Don't downplay it, compare it with other risks or pooh-pooh it; acknowledge that there is a risk of pollution, accident etc. Second, explain how and what management are doing to prevent problems *and* how they would cope with a 'disaster'. Third, stress that progression is more important, practical and realistic than perfection. The British, at any rate, prefer people to be disarmingly self-critical. It is better to say that one is trying hard and, every day in every way, striving for minor improvements. Fourth, indeed throughout the process, build trust. Only the Almighty is omniscient, omnipresent and omnipotent. The more that scientists, experts and consultants try to emulate Him, the more they fail.

You build trust by being human – that is the appeal of the soap star, the sporting hero and the TV presenter. They appear human and genuine.

The bottom line comes from the world of psychological counselling. Counsellors are trained to focus not on what people are saying, but on the emotion underlying the words. They are encouraged to explore and accept that emotion (fear, anxiety, anger) irrespective of whether it is reasonable or not. It is wrong to question the emotion, but it is worth exploring by reflecting it back to the patient. Indeed, counsellors might wallow too much in the emotional mud. But one has to respond to these emotions *before* getting into the rational arguments, and most scientists are not trained to do so.

37. Consultant Jargon is Pretty Easy to Understand

One way of being creative is to think through the opposite of an idea or technique. Academics have performed this trick so often that they have the triadic jargon terms of thesis, antithesis and synthesis.

Turning an idea on its head (as Marx did to Hegel) can be didactically useful, mischievous or just plain fun. It can help define positions or poles, clarify differences and set out clear alternatives. It can also point out the sheer ordinariness or commonsensical nature of ideas or concepts, because the opposites are so ridiculous. In a sense antonyms simply don't exist. Thus the opposite of looking for zero defects is to look for zero perfects or 100% defects.

Some opposites are not that obvious. Thus the opposite of managing by walking about (MBWA) could be management by staying in the office (MBSITO) or management by hiding away (MBHA) – surely more fun. But 'creative opposites' is a fun and useful exercise. Thus we have:

1. *Shoddy squares*: Sitting around in circular groups becoming obsessed with quality might be desirable for the anal obsessive but it is an incredible bore. Checking for, and throwing out, the odd shoddy product (or service system) is probably a good idea but not worth getting excited about.
2. *Disempowerment*: Because responsibility and accountability come with power, so does stress. Empowerment means nobody to blame; being on call; making executive decisions; and facing the consequences of one's actions. Disempowerment means the easy life and the old adage: 'I was merely following orders....'
3. *Relayering the company*: All this down- or rightsizing has been too similar to a vicious cull of the herd. Just as the mature

elephants are the embodiment of the wisdom of the herd, so we need to bring back the middle-brow middle manager and have a deep gateau of management layers to pad out the management structure.

4. *Thriving on order:* Organisations, like the world in general, are too chaotic, capricious and unpredictable to be either enjoyable or beneficial. Management's job is to give order to the organisation, to bring stability into the chances and changes of this fleeting world and to abolish chaos.

5. *De-engineering the organisation:* People are not machines and to talk in this language only encourages mechanistic thinking. Re-engineering is not the best metaphor in these people-oriented times. It is too redolent of the dark satanic mills of the last century. Perhaps a culinary metaphor should be used: 'Reheating the organisation' or 'Defrosting the organisation'.

6. *Job impoverishment:* All that consultant cost and claptrap of job enrichment ignores the obvious fact that it is not the tedious or routine nature of jobs that makes them distasteful, but having to do them at all. Job impoverishment removes horrid jobs. Get everyone to write down on a piece of paper the job they hate the most. Put these in a hat and draw one each to be performed next month. The same work gets done and everyone gets to do a new task.

7. *Management without objectives:* The trouble with MBO is that it expends massive and wasteful effort defining and then measuring objectives. Ignore mission statements; section goals; job descriptions. Work relations are optimised under MWO because people love doing their own thing. This is especially true of more senior positions where the undesirable side-effects of lower productivity are of little consequence.

8. *Time-serving related pay:* Performance-related pay means that loyalty to the organisation (40 years at the mast) is not sufficiently rewarded. Young, workaholic, thrusting newcomers get promoted over the steady-as-you-go types. Hence one needs to stop rewarding effort and ability and instead support LIFO (last in, first out) and FIGS (first in gets support). We could have one hour (not one minute) managers; corporate philistinism, not corporate culture.

The Blessed Margaret, as Lord St John Stevas described our ex-Prime Minister, understood the power of coming up with opposites.

In that strident, high-pitched, Boadicea-reminiscent voice she would turn with contempt on the cowed Labour parliamentarian and shout 'There Is No Alternative'. She knew, or hoped, that the available alternatives had either been tried before (and found wanting) or were clearly impractical.

Perhaps one could try shouting 'Creative Realistic Alternative Plans' (or its acronym) at board meetings or training sessions and see the immediate beneficial effects on the organisation.

38. Fame in Management Comes from Describing Secrets of Success

People or products whose name gets adopted as a verb or a noun achieve a particular form of fame. McAdam, for example, lent his name to road-tarring (to Macadamise the highway) and Australian nuts (Macadamias).

Certain brands live forever, in that one Hoovers the carpet and Sellotapes the parcel. Americans, it is said, believe in the inalienable right of all nouns to become verbs. Thus 'auto-condimentation' of food is putting the salt and pepper on it yourself. The ideal situation for inventors and those after fame is when proper nouns, i.e. their surnames, get adopted into the language.

Occasionally people lend their names to principles and laws which enshrine succinctly an idea or a kernel of truth. The world of management is surprisingly rich in such eponymous laws. What most have in common, though, is their scepticism about the folly of the human condition. Furthermore they frequently inspire numerous corollaries.

Consider the following five:

1. *Parkinson's Law.* This states quite simply that work expands to fill the time available for its completion. The law was based on the observation that managers seek to multiply subordinates, not rivals (and succeed in doing so); and that they tend to make work for one another. Management preference, it seems, leads to payroll obesity rather than anorexia. Some managers even believe that if they don't get complaints about overwork, the Parkinson syndrome has struck. It is precisely because of the operation of this law that re-engineering, delayering, rightsizing and other synonymous activities meet with such resistance and are so necessary.

2. *The Peter Principle.* This observes that in a hierarchical organisa-

tion every employee tends to rise to his level of incompetence. The idea is that in any reward-based system those who do well are pushed up till they get a job beyond their abilities and competence and thus are no longer eligible for rewards. Performance in one job is confused with potential in another (the next one up). Thus it is often the case that technical experts (scientists, engineers) are promoted to managerial jobs that they both hate and are hopeless at.

3.   *The Pareto Principle.* This has been adapted from an economic observation about the distribution of wealth to become the 80:20 rule: 20% of the variables (vital few) influence 80% (trivial many) of the results. Analysing a cause–effect situation makes it possible to isolate key factors (positive or negative) for remedial action. And either the vital few or trivial many may hold the secret of improvement. This is one case where managers can get results by dealing with the vital few causes of excessive absenteeism, whereas in a cost-cutting exercise it is the excessive expenditure on the trivial many that requires action.

4.   *The Zeigarnik Effect.* This refers to the tendency of workers to resist interruption. In the words of a now-famous quizmaster 'I have started, so I will finish'. It tends to explain why some employees work late, with no overtime, to complete a project in which they are involved. It also 'explains' why employees sometimes balk at stopping one task and starting another, even one with much higher priorities. The Zeigarnik effect is the addiction of the completer-finisher and the grave of the prioritiser.

5.   *Machiavellian Power Principles.* It is to this 16th-century consultant to the crowned heads of Europe that we owe the idea 'better to be feared than loved'. It is better to be parsimonious than generous and better to be known for cunning than ethical behaviour. Machiavellians strive for a desirable reputation, believing that is sufficient. Duplicity and audacity are thought of not so much as desirable characteristics but as the necessities of being a manager.

There are other eponymous concepts in management. Everyone knows Murphy's rule(s) 'When anything can go wrong it will'; 'Nothing is as easy as it looks'; 'Everything takes longer than you expect'.

But why is it that eponymous fame comes to management thinkers only when they codify human foibles and not when they celebrate human kindness, worker motivation and organisational efficiency? Possibly because we only *learn* from our mistakes and not from our successes; possibly because when an organisation is successful nobody remembers but when it fails nobody forgets. Possibly because management scientists are exclusively cynics.

39. Staff Surveys Give Clear Answers

Polls show the public to be hypocritical and contradictory in their opinions. In that possibly portentous mini-saga 'To Play the King', the fictional Prime Minister's rather-too-sexy 'adviser' pointed out that by subtle wording of opinion-poll questions, one could always obtain the results one wanted.

Managers increasingly commission climate and culture surveys which require employees to agree or disagree with various statements about their perception of the company. Can these questions be skilfully worded by managers to give the answers they want to hear? And how do employees react when they can 'see through' the motives of the questionnaire writer and don't agree with his/her point of view? There may be another method.

Consider opinion polls about tax. Almost everyone believes he/she is being overtaxed and that taxation should be reduced; but at the same time everyone wants more money spent on health, education, crime prevention etc. Of course, one could argue that these ideas are not incompatible. For instance, the government could increase indirect taxation as opposed to income tax, to raise revenue whilst leaving people more discretion in their spending habits. Or one could argue that 'the rich' should be heavily taxed, but not oneself. This 'politics-of-envy' thinking is very popular in Britain because whoever you are (say, a Labour MP on about £40 000 plus perks), you never include yourself among those to be taxed more highly.

But, alas, the great British public – or any public for that matter – are not so sophisticated. Various studies have shown that in opinion surveys people *are* contradictory. For example, an American polling company reported that 63% of people agreed with the view that 'When 12 000 air-traffic controllers are willing to sacrifice their careers and economic security, and even go to jail, there must be some legitimate reasons for their going on strike'. The same poll found that 69% supported the opinion that 'Since every air-traffic controller took an oath not to strike, President Reagan was right to fire them'. Obviously, a lot of people must have agreed with both statements, revealing nothing about whether or not they supported the strike.

The writing of opinion items, then, is itself highly political. And it is not good science. So some psychologists have cast about for other approaches. One solution was to reduce the item down to its central core, adopting a familiar catch-phrase to represent the issue, and reserving all evaluation for the response alternatives. The formula 'X is a good/bad thing considering Y and Z' (agree or disagree?) was replaced by the simpler formula: 'X' (good or bad?). This, they believed, would tap immediate emotional reactions to controversial issues, and would be closer to actual behavioural dispositions.

The technique is to abandon the propositional form of an item, and instead simply present a list of brief labels or 'catch-phrases' representing various familiar and controversial issues. It is assumed that, in the course of previous conversation and argument concerning these issues, the respondent has already placed him- or herself in relation to the general population, and is able to indicate his/her 'position' immediately and simply.

It is easy to demonstrate. Ask a group to write a 5000-word essay on capital punishment and have two judges to assess whether they are, on balance, 'for', 'uncertain' or 'against'. And ask the essay writers also to complete the catch-phrase poll. The results are nearly identical, saving the time and effort of the lengthier approach. The propositional approach demands that the interviewee provides instant appraisal of complex and authoritatively worded statements of opinion: the catch-phrase is believed to tap into immediate emotional reactions to controversial issues and is closer to actual behavioural dispositions.

Furthermore, this technique overcomes many of the problems of grammatical confusion and social desirability. Why not try it and see? I have constructed a simple economic beliefs scale.

Economic Beliefs

Which of the following do you favour or believe in? Circle Yes or No. If truly uncertain, circle (?). There are no right or wrong answers. Do not discuss them; just give your first reaction. Answer all items.

1. Nationalisation	Yes	?	No
2. Self-sufficiency	Yes	?	No
3. Socialism	Yes	?	No

4.	Free market	Yes	?	No
5.	Trade unions	Yes	?	·No
6.	Saving	Yes	?	No
7.	Closed shops	Yes	?	No
8.	Monetarism	Yes	?	No
9.	Import controls	Yes	?	No
10.	Privatisation	Yes	?	No
11.	Strikes	Yes	?	No
12.	Informal black economy	Yes	?	No
13.	Inheritance tax	Yes	?	No
14.	Insurance schemes	Yes	?	No
15.	Council housing	Yes	?	No
16.	Private schools	Yes	?	No
17.	Child benefits	Yes	?	No
18.	Profit	Yes	?	No
19.	Wealth tax	Yes	?	No
20.	Public spending cuts	Yes	?	No

Scoring: odd items   Yes = 3, ? = 2, No = 1
           even items   Yes = 1, ? = 2, No = 3

Score 50 to 70 and you are what my father would call a 'dangerous pinko'. **Score 20 to 30** and my students would call you an economic fascist. **Score 31 to 40** and you are probably a member of the entrepreneurial neo-right. **Score 41 to 50** and you are probably a wobbly liberal.

Pedants, pollsters and politicians would probably object to this method. But pundits and the public would welcome it because of its simplicity. Opinion polling is not 'rocket science' but it is a lot better than reading the tea-leaves, or worse, horoscopes. It does have its uses and many amongst the media are addicted to them. The catch-phrase method may indeed be superior to and simpler than our more established methods.

40. Travel Broadens the Mind

For many people the summer always heralds the package holiday so indulgently mulled over and decided upon in the dark, damp, winter. But the air journey itself is often the least enjoyable part of the holiday: unpleasant and uncomfortable and involving long hours of waiting, sitting in cramped conditions, being shepherded uncomprehendingly around for no apparent reason, being served with tasteless, barely edible food. There is no doubt that air travel is one of the least pleasant forms of journeying and this can paradoxically be most clearly seen from the many airline advertisements in magazines, the newspapers and on television.

All airline advertisements can be categorised into two broad categories: the *Big Lie* approach vs the *Exotic Destination* appeal. The former clearly learned from *der Führer* when he noted in *Mein Kampf*: 'The broad mass of a nation...will more easily fall victim to a big lie than to a small one', and hence instead of even approximating the truth they tell the very opposite – a whopping fib. The exotic destination theme is clearly teleological, assuming that analysis of, and subsequent commitment to, the end (the tropical destination) automatically generates relaxing or at least acceptable means to achieve it. Thus one ignores the means (of travel) and stresses the end (the destination).

The big lie approach has numerous variants. Some advertisements stress the new wide, retracting, supportive seats that are *wider* than those of any other airline. Some even detail the various aspects of the *new, super-reclining, controllable* chair which bears a justifiable similarity to a dentist's chair. Indeed a visit to the dentist and a flight have much in common – they are both expensive, painful, sterilised and aimed at reducing one into a passive, dependent, incommunicative object. Of course, one could argue that if God had wanted us to travel tourist class he would have made us narrower. A second variant of the big lie approach offers a hint of sex and seduction. Far Eastern airlines attempt to persuade one that a flight on one of their jets bears a close similarity to a visit to a massage parlour. Seductively shy, here-to-grant-your-every-wish, slant-eyed goddesses smile with satisfaction at the clearly relaxed (relief-massaged?) western businessman reclining in the warm womb-like cabin. Another advertisement seems to imply that the passengers are having so much fun on board that when the plane lands they choose not to disembark into the terminal but to kick balloons erratically out of the door as a sign of having such fun. One rule (of very many) infringed by passengers is the releasing of safety belts and heading for the door while the plane is still taxiing to the destination terminal. All want to escape as soon as possible.

The exotic destination appeal makes no pretence that air travel is comfortable, sexy or fun. In fact it ignores all aspects of the flight, preferring to show people the outstanding (and usually wholly unrepresentative) features of their proposed destination. Furthermore these destinations must be Europeanised and, like all general travel brochures, must include Hockneyesque blue–green seas and bleached-white beaches, requiring the wearing of sunglasses, and sparse evidence of a few opulent, beautiful people. The occasional symbol of the country or continent may also be required (the Taj Mahal for India; Sydney Opera House for Australia; a lion for any part of Africa, etc). The message is that by flying (usually the national) airline one may indulge in the joys, sights, and smells of the destination. No mention of free drinks, wide seats or sexy airline stewardesses here.

Why is airline travel so uncomfortable and unpleasant? The predominant reason is not the cost, the restricted space, the tasteless food, but the fact that one becomes carefully institutionalised into a flying privatised prison. The term 'total institution' was first used by the sociologist Erving Goffman in 1964, referring to institutions such as schools, prisons, mental hospitals, army camps etc. which have rigid routines, block treatment and systems of depersonalisation. The film *One Flew Over the Cuckoo's Nest* explored the idea of what a total institution does to the individual. Goffman mentioned five types of social institution: those established to care for persons felt to be incapable and harmless (old-age homes, orphanages); those established to care for those incapable of looking after themselves *and* posing a threat to the community (TB sanatoriums, mental hospitals); those organised to protect the community against what are thought to be intentional dangers to it (gaols, POW camps); those institutions which justify themselves on instrumental grounds in pursuing some task (army barracks, boarding schools); and those establishments designed as retreats from the world – and possibly training institutes (abbeys, convents). A sixth is, in my view, an aircraft cabin.

Consider the similarities between going to prison and flying in an international aeroplane. First, one is *deprived of one's possessions*. Nearly all one's possessions are inspected (by X-ray) and removed, sometimes never to be returned. One is thus left metaphorically naked, helpless and deprived of the security of familiar, often practical objects. Second, one is *given a number*. The depersonalisation process occurs right from the beginning – one may start off being passenger Smith, but more frequently the boarding card is one's number, one's identity. Very soon one is thought of as 17c: non-smoking aisle seat, club class, paid-by-credit-card. The number is one's label, one's identity and people soon comply by saying, for instance, 'I'm 46d, who are you?'. Third, one is encouraged to be *strapped into one's seat* – often, it seems, simply to keep one under control. Apparently for 'one's safety and comfort' one may like to keep the belt on for the duration of the trip. Of course this limits mobility and access, both of which are crucially important in every institution – for safety, of course. Fourth, in some parts of the world one is actually *sanitised*. Strange-looking health inspectors sometimes walk up and down the aisles like thurifers spraying the faithful. Again, like de-lousing procedures, this is for one's protection. Fifth, meals are served to everybody at the same time, there being often *no choice*. Ideally the meals are served for the convenience of the institution, not the comfort of the passengers. Thus one is likely to receive meals at set times, or indeed be deprived of food, which bears no relation to one's actual needs. Of course, everybody gets the same food (though much is made of what limited choice there is) in a strict (often cost-of-seat-based) order. Drinks are served much like Valium in a hospital or sleeping pills in a hospice, not for the comfort or indulgence of the travellers but for the power this gives the staff. A drugged inmate is an easy inmate. Sixth, there are *many rules* to be obeyed. These are flashed at one, told to one and provided in writing. They are not justified, except under the general banner of 'for your own safety'. They extend to sitting, standing, walking, defecating and smoking, and are politely but strictly enforced.

But most of all one is always *deprived of information*. The prevailing bureaucracy demands that one *provides* extensive details of oneself – before and after the flight – but one is rarely *given* information. This begins long before boarding the plane. The initial and crucial period of disorientation starts up to an hour before boarding. A series of televised or loud-speaker (in both senses of the word) announcements force one to move from one waiting room to another, each being smaller and more barren than the former. One's papers are checked repeatedly: tickets, passports, boarding card, disembarkation certificates must all be produced for different people. By the time one enters the plane – by section, often called out by number (rows 16–20) – the dehumanisation process has begun. One should not believe, however, that one is never given any information. In fact on nearly every flight a jovial captain tells one the speed and altitude of the aircraft, the weather conditions, the title of the in-flight movie and a range of often trivial facts that rarely relate to the traveller's needs. The problem with the information that one receives is twofold. First, one often doubts that it is true – just as doctors may be tempted not to tell the anxious (extremely ill or at least with a poor prognosis) patient the whole (or indeed even part) of the truth – so one often suspects the captain and stewardess choose their words to soothe, calm or prevent anxiety, or at least only present palatable parts of the truth. All disaster and spoof disaster movies support this point. Second, the information one is supplied with has been simplified for the hard-of-thinking. It is patronisingly assumed that one's ability to understand mechanical, meteorological or bureaucratic problems is minimal and that all this should be left to experts. Information is power, is control and in an institutionalised environment one must be deprived of it and of access to it.

To embark upon air travel, then, is to enter an institution where one is processed and de-individualised; rendered passive and helpless; and ruthlessly if smilingly controlled by the staff.

It is no accident that the words travel and travail are etymologically linked, for the two frequently co-occur. Indeed it is probably true to invert the old adage: it is better to arrive than to travel hopefully. Generally it seems as if long flights in cramped institutionalised jets serve only to broaden the behind and not the mind!

Index

Printed and bound by CPI Group (UK) Ltd, Croydon, CR0 4YY

10/06/2024

14512910-0001